What People are saying about....

The Discipleship Dare

Dr. George O. Wood

General Superintendent of the General Council of the Assemblies of God | Springfield, Missouri

The Discipleship Dare is a challenging, worthwhile 40-day journey through the risks of discipling. Each day the reader has opportunity to analyze himself or herself, apply the truths learned, and pray a prayer of intentionality.

Dr. Don Meyer

President of Valley Forge Christian College | Phoenixville, Pennsylvania

Christian leaders are always looking for tools which can be used for their own personal journey, but also which can be given to those whom they are mentoring in the faith. Jess Bousa's *The Discipleship Dare* book is such a resource. Here you will find an extremely practicable, easily readable, well laid out and presented guide for growing in the faith. I will want many of them within reach for use in my own ministry. I commend this to you with highest recommendations.

Rev. Joseph S. Batluck Sr., D.Min, CH (COL) USA-Ret.

President/Executive Director of Teen Challenge Training Center, Inc. | Rehrersburg, Pennsylvania

Dietrich Bonhoffer in *The Cost of Discipleship* said, "When Christ calls a man, he bids him come and die." The paradox of life springing from death is captured by Rev. Bousa. Jess beckons all believers—cautious, careful, crazy—to dare to be God's person through a life of passionate, Christ-centered discipline. The reader will live in a new way as he dies again.

Dr. Mark Reynolds

Associate Director of Redeemer Church Planting Center | New York, New York

Bousa has developed an excellent resource for church planters across the country. *The Discipleship Dare* is a challenging devotional for new believers and mature Christians alike. The risk of discipleship is worth it. Take the Dare!

Rev. Rich Cortese

Senior Pastor of Garden City Church | Beverly, Massachusetts

The Discipleship Dare by Jess Bousa has been a tremendous blessing to our congregation and to me personally. Each devotional is thought-provoking, challenging and extremely practical. It is full of great insights and realistic truth that will help any follower of Christ know what it means to be a disciple. My suggestion: read it! I dare you.

Rev. Derrick Smith

Church Planter of Kaleidoscope Ethnic Fellowship | Spartanburg, South Carolina

The Discipleship Dare is a great way to get a large or small group on the same page when it comes to discipleship. It will teach and challenge the seeker, the new believer, and the mature Christian alike to become a more fully committed follower of Jesus Christ. Its daily bite-sized devotional morsels are Scriptural and relevant. Take the dare.

Bishop Doc Loomis

Missionary Bishop of The Anglican Mission in the Americas | Medina, Ohio

Bousa's devotional guide to taking on the daily risk of being a follower of Christ, fully engaged in mission, is an invaluable tool for every Christian. I highly recommend it as a powerful daily guide for your Christian walk.

Dr. Tom Cocklereece

Author of Simple Discipleship | Marietta, GA

With his book, *The Discipleship Dare*, Jess Bousa has helped churches build "chosen accountability" into their cultures by leading whole congregations to grow together in their spiritual vitality. Don't just read it...read and discuss it together in small groups and watch your church grow in spiritual depth and in number.

Dr. Samuel R. Schutz

Gordon-Conwell Theological Seminary Professor of Evangelism and Ministry | South Hamilton, Massachusetts

Bousa's *Discipleship Dare* is an excellent introduction of what it means to be an authentic Christian within the church and in ministry to the larger community. Eminently practical, thoroughly biblical, and ideal for individuals or small groups.

Rev. David Pilch

Director of Syracuse Teen Challenge | Syracuse, New York

I really like how Jess is able to draw the reader in...practical and powerful. An excellent tool to re-fire Christians.

The Discipleship Dare

Living Dangerously for God

Jess Bousa

TREMENDOUS LIFE BOOKS.com

206 West Allen Street
Mechanicsburg, PA 17055
1-800-233-2665

The Discipleship Dare: Living Dangerously for God

Published by
Tremendous Life Books
206 West Allen Street
Mechanicsburg, PA 17055

ISBN: 978-1-933715-96-4

Cover Concept and Interior Design by Ron Kline

Printed in the United States of America

To My Dad,
the first one to dare me to follow Christ

CONTENTS

Section Three - The Commissioning of a Disciple

Section Four - The Community Life of a Disciple

What if the Biggest Risk in Life is Never Taking Any Risk at All?

FOREWORD

What better way to tackle the subject of discipleship than one day at a time?

Jess Bousa "dares" you to try this approach and see what transpires after 40 days in the following material. If you're anything like me, it can take multiple readings before a holistic understanding of discipleship really sinks in. But, when you see what Jess has provided for you in his own words, add in the Scriptures, prayer and practical application, and you're holding in your hands an invaluable resource!

Discipleship is all about becoming more and more like Christ. We who are his followers are *little Christs*, growing up to become more and more like Christ, in order that others may discover the joy of following him too. Since we are multi-faceted individuals, the principles we are invited to follow are many and varied. This 40-day "dare" will get you into many important aspects of your spiritual life and your service to others. Unlike other materials, this devotional approach will lead you through one important piece of discipleship after another. As you soak in the Word and prayer, invite God to speak to you and inform both your mind and your will.

Taking the dare seriously will lead you into receiving in your heart the best gift of all—a deeper intimacy with Jesus Christ. His invitation is for you to come close, draw near, and follow Him. I join the author in daring you to take Jesus up on his offer of an abundant life. You'll be so glad you did.

Grateful for the joy of the journey,

A fellow disciple,

Stephen A. Macchia, D.Min.

Founder and President, Leadership Transformations, Inc.

Author, Becoming A Healthy Church and *Becoming A Healthy Disciple*

PROLOGUE
THE RISK OF DISCIPLESHIP

"The person who risks nothing, does nothing, has nothing,
is nothing, and becomes nothing. He may avoid suffering
and sorrow, but he simply cannot learn and feel and
change and grow and love and live."
Leo F. Buscaglia

Discipleship is *risky*.

There is a lot of risk involved, but as the saying goes, "The greater the risks, the greater the rewards." When was the last time you took a risk? When was the last time you were "all in?" We take risks all the time. We take financial risks by not living within our means, but within our dreams. We risk money in the stock market, the real estate market and with credit card companies. We risk our physical well-being by eating unhealthy food and not exercising regularly. We risk our intellects by allowing movies, television, and music to shape our views on life. The last area people tend to take great risk in is their relationship with God. What if we have neglected to take risks in the most important area of life? What if the biggest risk in life is not taking any for the cause of Christ at all?

Discipleship is *challenging*.

Life is challenging. The amount of challenge you face will determine the kind of life you live. Some people thrive in the face of challenge, others are just happy to survive. Marines are challenged to thrive at all times no matter the costs. There are two places in America where men are turned into Marines: Paris Island, South Carolina and San Diego, California. Every year approximately 38,000 Marines receive their basic training, which is far more challenging than any other branch of the military. According to John Seel, most Marines

testify that going through the twelve weeks of boot camp to gain entrance into the most elite armed forces is the most challenging thing they ever had to do in their lives. Marines are significantly challenged, both intellectually and physically, but often not spiritually. What does it profit you to be challenged in every area of life except spirituality, causing you to lose your own soul in the process?

Discipleship is *training.*

Discipleship is the training process where men and women are made into fully devoted followers of Christ. Disciples must heed the same warning new Marine recruits are given by their drill sergeants. Even though basic training is hard, it's not nearly as hard as being a Marine. The training, for all of its high intensity and great challenge, is only training. Like basic training, discipleship prepares you for war. As a disciple, you can endure any attack physically if you are spiritually equipped. There is nothing anyone can do to jeopardize your calling as a disciple. Your training as a disciple is the foundation upon which all of life's ups and downs rest. It is the one stable, consistent area of life that is unshakable, unbreakable, and impenetrable by the attacks of the enemy. It is the place in life that produces an everlasting joy and a quality of life that is unmatched by the satisfaction of wealth, status, or power. What if some of the training we received in life led us to do good things, but hindered us from the training that would have led us to do great things?

The life Jesus lived is worth dying for. You have not really lived until you have lived a life worth dying for. Jesus lived, died, and conquered death not for His benefit, but for yours. He changed the course of history forever by dying for a life worth living, a life other people died for as they followed His example. Would anybody die for the life you live? Is your life worth modeling? Do you live a lifestyle that transforms the people around you? Robert Schuller once said, "No person is truly alive until he has found a cause he is willing to die for." There is not a cause on this planet more worthy of your life than God's global mission.

Discipleship is a *dare*.

Jesus dared His first disciples thousands of years ago to follow Him. The invitation still stands today. *The Discipleship Dare* is for all Christ followers, no matter whether a babe in Christ or a veteran believer. Every follower of Christ needs a regular discipleship tune-up. Discipleship is not easy. It requires a serious investment of time. There is nothing like the reward of knowing that you are living like Jesus, the Son of God, who died on the cross to restore the world through discipleship. He did not take it lightly and neither should His disciples.

Each day of this journey will include three very significant parts:

First, a quote, scripture passage, and devotional will be introduced. Don't skip reading the passage. It is important to read the devotion with the passage in mind. The devotion is an explanation of the passage meant to challenge you to consider the dare.

Then, you will be challenged to respond each day to a specific dare. There are many kinds of dares: commitment dares, character dares, etc. After you complete the first part and read the dare for the day, be courageous enough to prayerfully consider it. Each dare builds on the previous dare.

Finally, you will be challenged to do a personal bible study on the day's passage. Wayne Cordeiro invented the S.O.A.P. Bible study tool for hearing from God. S.O.A.P. stands for scripture, observation, application, and prayer. The passage will be provided each day. Meditate on a portion of it. Memorize favorite parts at your own pace. Ask and answer two questions of the passage and pray to close your time.

Remember, God has called you to be in relationship with Him. God's Word is the primary means by which He speaks to us today. Learn to love His Word as you respond to His call. Disciples are learners. If you commit to being an excellent student of His word, then you will be a great disciple.

Section 1

The Calling of a Disciple

DAY 1
Follow Me

"God does not call the qualified, he qualifies the called."
Anonymous Author

As Jesus was walking beside the Sea of Galilee, He saw two brothers, Simon called Peter and his brother Andrew. They were casting a net into the lake, for they were fishermen. "Come, follow me," Jesus said, "and I will make you fishers of men." At once they left their nets and followed Him. Going on from there, He saw two other brothers, James son of Zebedee and his brother John. They were in a boat with their father Zebedee, preparing their nets. Jesus called them, and immediately they left the boat and their father and followed Him. —Matthew 4:18-22

Jesus invites you to follow Him and calls His followers to enlist others in His worldwide mission on earth. His invitation is not limited to you in your corner of the world, but is for everyone, throughout the world. It is a global invitation to all people in all nations. When Jesus asked the first disciples to join Him, He did not have in mind a local community organization but a global movement. Jesus' plan to reach the world began with an invitation—a dare to change the world.

Jesus' invitation to those first disciples was an extraordinary act of love. He went against the ordinary process first-century teachers used when choosing disciples. Traditionally, disciples were hand-selected by teachers. They were chosen based on past performance. But Jesus chose His disciples based on future potential. Jesus believed in His squad before they believed in themselves. He did not pick them because they were qualified. If they were qualified for the job, they would not have been working as ordinary fishermen. They would have already been following a teacher of the law, which is a rabbi.

Jesus does not take our past religious resume into consideration when He calls us to partner with Him in His mission to restore the world. He calls us based on His resume. He died for the sins of the world. His death activated God's grace—His undeserved favor for life. We do not deserve to be part of Jesus' international movement, but have been privileged with the opportunity. By accepting His invitation to follow Him, you are enlisting into active duty. The mission of God is to seek and save those who are broken by bringing restoration to relationships in all directions: God, self, others and the world. If you have already been active in His mission, your role remains the same, but your responsibility does not. You are responsible to enlist others into active duty, not by force, but by love.

Men and women who first join the Marines are untrained and not physically fit for the mission. The military understands this dynamic, but also knows that as long as the new recruits are committed to the mission, they will become Marines. In the same way, Jesus invites ordinary people into a partnership with Him in order to launch them out to do extraordinary things in all parts of the world. Jesus' mission is to change the world. If you are committed to the mission of God on earth, then you will become a fully devoted follower of Christ who is a catalyst of change and an example of human goodness; an agent of change in your neighborhood, family, workplace, and church.

TODAY'S *Commitment* DARE

The first commitment dare is simple, but not easy. Jesus dares you to follow Him. Today, prayerfully resolve to join God's worldwide mission by accepting His invitation to follow Him no matter where He leads and no matter who He leads you to enlist.

TODAY'S *S.O.A.P.* STUDY

Scripture:

Matthew 4:18-21 Read, Write & Memorize

_____

_____

_____

_____

_____

_____

_____

Observation:

What is God speaking to my heart as I read?

_____

_____

_____

_____

_____

_____

_____

TODAY'S *S.O.A.P.* STUDY

Application:

How does this truth apply to my call to follow Jesus?

_____

_____

_____

_____

_____

_____

Prayer:

In light of what God has shown me, how do I need to pray?

_____

_____

_____

_____

_____

_____

DAY 2
Deny Yourself

"Jesus calls us to say no to ourselves so we can say yes to Him."
Greg Ogden

Then He called the crowd to Him along with His disciples and said: "If anyone would come after me, he must deny himself and take up his cross and follow me."—Mark 8:34

Jesus never sugarcoated any of His teachings. He was upfront with all people at all times. In the gospel of Mark, Jesus shares with us the terms and conditions of discipleship for those wanting to join His international movement (Mark 8:34). These are extremely important. You don't want to move forward without understanding them, because the way you understand Jesus' call will determine the way you live it out. If you are a veteran follower of Christ, but live a life not marked by great sacrifice, then revisit and reclaim these fundamentals of the Christian faith in your own life.

Marines make great sacrifices when training for combat, because they are expected to make great sacrifices in combat. If becoming a Marine is not a great sacrifice, then living as a Marine will not be full of great sacrifice. It is the same for someone who wants to become a disciple of Christ. If a disciple does not make great sacrifices joining God's movement, then He will not live a life of great sacrifice for His movement. The degree of commitment made when a disciple first responds to Jesus' invitation will impact the degree of commitment with which the disciple lives out his or her faith.

The first term and condition of discipleship is self-denial. Following Jesus begins with denying yourself lordship of your life. Greg Ogden comments on this in his book, *Discipleship Essentials:* "It means saying no to the god who is me, to reject the demands of the god who is me, to refuse to obey the claims of the god who is me." There is only room for one person on the throne of your life. Jesus alone must occupy the throne. His plans for the restoration of the world, not your plans for your life, must be the priority. God's plan is bigger than any plan you might have for your life. It impacts every inch of the planet. Every people group, culture, and society is impacted by His plan. At the core of His plan is selflessness, in opposition to the heart of our plans which is selfishness. Jesus knows it is impossible to try to live out both His plan and ours. Living out God's plan does not mean your daily life will dramatically change, but that you will give God the opportunity to use you at your place of work, at home, in your neighborhood, or in your school. This radical first step must be taken, if you are to fully experience the abundant life Jesus came, lived, and conquered death for.

TODAY'S *Commitment* DARE

The second commitment dare sets the stage for the next five. Jesus dares you to deny yourself and make Him Lord of your life. Today, prayerfully resolve to live out God's plan for your life no matter how He leads.

TODAY'S *S. O. A. P.* STUDY

Scripture:

Mark 8:34 Read, Write & Memorize

_____

_____

_____

_____

_____

_____

Observation:

What is God speaking to my heart as I read?

_____

_____

_____

_____

_____

_____

TODAY'S *S.O.A.P.* STUDY

Application:

How does this truth apply to my call to follow Jesus?

_____

_____

_____

_____

_____

_____

Prayer:

In light of what God has shown me, how do I need to pray?

_____

_____

_____

_____

_____

_____

DAY 3
Take up Your Cross

*"A sacrifice to be real must cost,
must hurt, must empty ourselves."*

Mother Teresa

*"And anyone who does not carry his cross and follow me cannot be
my disciple."*—Luke 14:27

In the military, the more sacrifice new recruits make in training, the more prepared they will be in combat. Out of shape, undisciplined, untrained soldiers will not succeed in combat. Recruits need to sacrifice their personal agenda for the agenda of the military's mission. The role of drill instructors is to scare the fear of death out of recruits and place a purpose of mission in them.

The greatest sacrifice anyone could ever make on earth is to give up one's life so that others can gain life. Jesus Christ sacrificed His life not only for those who accepted Him but for those who rejected Him. There was not an area in Jesus' life that was without sacrifice. At times, He sacrificed food, money, and shelter. He even gave up his life for the sake of others. The life he lived left a legacy of one who made great sacrifice. He selflessly gave His entire life for the mission of God on earth.

The mission of God on the earth is unstoppable. It is not dependent on any one person but on God. The mystery of the mission is that God partners with people to accomplish it. It requires a life of sacrifice. If a soldier is not willing to do whatever it takes, including dying, then the mission will fail. If Jesus were not willing to die for God's mission, then it would not have been accomplished. His selfless death showed

His disciples that God's mission is worth living for on earth. Followers of Christ who embrace the mission understand the importance of making sacrifices for its advancement.

The second term and condition of discipleship is self-sacrifice. Jesus challenges anyone who follows Him to live life carrying a cross. Literally speaking, in the ancient world, the cross was carried by condemned criminals to their place of execution as crowds lined the way hurling abuse at them. Their lives were open for the public's scrutiny. Figuratively speaking, in today's world, the cross is carried by committed disciples to their workplaces, in their neighborhoods or anywhere else they go, making our lifestyles open to others. The lifestyle of a disciple is not something to hide. Jesus calls His followers to live a life of open discipleship. People can't persecute you if they don't know you are a disciple of Christ, and they can't follow you as you follow Christ if they don't know you are a disciple. The greatest sacrifice you can make is to live a life marked with great sacrifice. Only then will people see Jesus in you.

TODAY'S *Commitment* DARE

The third commitment dare builds on the previous one. Jesus dares you to carry your cross openly through life. He calls you to live out your faith openly, not shrinking back from the criticism of others and not holding back from giving your life for others. Today, prayerfully resolve to live out God's plan for your life no matter who criticizes you for following Him.

TODAY'S *S.O.A.P.* STUDY

<u>S</u>cripture:

Luke 14:27 Read, Write & Memorize

_____

_____

_____

_____

_____

_____

<u>O</u>bservation:

What is God speaking to my heart as I read?

_____

_____

_____

_____

_____

_____

TODAY'S *S. O. A. P.* STUDY

Application:

How does this truth apply to my call to follow Jesus?

_____

_____

_____

_____

_____

_____

Prayer:

In light of what God has shown me, how do I need to pray?

_____

_____

_____

_____

_____

_____

DAY 4
Sell Your Possessions

"You give but little when you give of your possessions. It is when you give of yourself that you truly give."

Kahlil Gibran

Jesus answered, "If you want to be perfect, go, sell your possessions and give to the poor, and you will have treasure in heaven. Then come, follow me."—Matthew 19:21

This is one of the hardest sayings of Jesus to stomach in today's culture, a culture wrought with consumerism. Possessions are idolized and envied. If you are committed to living sacrificially, then the challenge might seem possible, but highly improbable. Do not worry. Jesus is not necessarily looking for you to sell everything you own. Following Christ will not automatically lead to poverty. For the rich young ruler who asked Jesus, "What good thing must I do to get eternal life?," Jesus said to Him, "obey the commandments" (Matthew 19:16-17). The rich young ruler admitted to keeping the latter five of the Ten Commandments, but purposely left the first five out. He only kept the commandments that had to do with his relationship with others publicly, like "Do not steal" or "Do not commit adultery" (Matthew 19:18), not those that had to do with his relationship with God privately.

At the heart of the matter was the man's love for God. The man who Jesus radically challenged loved his possessions more than anything else in life, including God. What is it that you love? What are you devoted to? If you love your possessions, then you're in trouble like this man. Jesus dares you to sell whatever comes between you and a self-denying, self-sacrificing relationship with God. In the military, new recruits are taught the importance of possessions. In combat, an overloaded or undersupplied backpack is detrimental to your survival. Carrying too many posses-

sions will endanger the survival of a soldier. Jesus requires His followers to pack light in regards to our loyalty to possessions. Possessions
can cause distractions. This leads to distance between you and God.
Where do your loyalties rest: with serving possessions or with serving
God? Do they rest in your bank account or in God? If your possessions
own you, then your loyalties are misdirected. The loyalty gap is bridged
when owning possessions becomes a non-issue and serving God becomes non-negotiable.

The third term and condition of discipleship is selflessness. The
more belongings and money you possess, the more sacrifice is required,
and the harder it is to deny yourself of your right to possess things. The
less you are able to live with, the more you will be able to give away.
The rich young ruler could not fathom living with less. Jesus' encounter
with him does not have a fairy-tale ending. After Jesus challenged the
rich young ruler to sell his possessions, "he went away sad, because He
had great wealth" (Matthew 19:22). The truth is, possessions and
money can hinder you from living a life of great sacrifice for the benefit
of others. Live with an open hand, not a tight grip on your possessions.

TODAY'S *Commitment* DARE

The fourth commitment dare builds on the
previous three. Jesus dares you to live
with less so that you can give more. He
dares you to get rid of anything that will
hinder you from loving God more. Today,
prayerfully resolve to live out God's plan
for your life no matter how much stuff
must be sold, returned, or given away.

TODAY'S *S. O. A. P.* STUDY

Scripture:

Matthew 19:21 Read, Write & Memorize

_____

_____

_____

_____

_____

_____

Observation:

What is God speaking to my heart as I read?

_____

_____

_____

_____

_____

TODAY'S *S.O.A.P.* STUDY

Application:

How does this truth apply to my call to follow Jesus?

_____

_____

_____

_____

_____

_____

Prayer:

In light of what God has shown me, how do I need to pray?

_____

_____

_____

_____

_____

_____

DAY 5

Hate

"Beware of anything that competes with loyalty to Jesus Christ."

Oswald Chambers

Large crowds were traveling with Jesus, and turning to them He said: "If anyone comes to me and does not hate his father and mother, his wife and children, his brothers and sisters—yes, even his own life—he cannot be my disciple."—Luke 14:25-26

The American Army has a code of conduct that all their soldiers must live by when on active duty. The first article of the code reads: "I am an American, fighting in the forces which guard my country and our way of life. I am prepared to give my life in their defense." The Army requires their soldiers to love their country more than their own lives. Soldiers must first pledge allegiance to the protection of America before they pledge it to their family, friends and/or vocation. A soldier's loyalties are based on the Army's mission, and in the same way the loyalties of disciples of Christ are based on God's mission.

The fourth term and condition of discipleship is switching allegiances. Similar to the Army, Jesus has a code of conduct for His followers. If His followers are not primarily loyal to Him, they can compromise God's mission on earth. Jesus does not literally mean His followers are to hate their families. Followers of Christ must first pledge their allegiance to God, not family, or their lifelong dreams and goals. Your love for Jesus must supersede whatever love you have for anything or anybody else, otherwise your partnership in God's mission will be undermined.

When civilians first join the Army, they undergo an extreme priority makeover. The makeover prepares them for their mission. The mission is impossible without total commitment to a priority shift and allegiance change. Once Army affairs become the priority over civilian affairs, then the mission becomes possible. In 2 Timothy 2:3-4, the apostle Paul challenges Timothy, a young disciple, with these words: "Endure hardship with us like a good soldier of Christ Jesus. No one serving as a soldier gets involved in civilian affairs—he wants to please his commanding officer." Single-minded devotion to the mission of God is required for greater impact for the mission of God.

Jesus is the commanding officer. It is only possible to please one person. There is no room in war for a soldier to switch allegiances or to switch priorities. People can die if soldiers waver. Jesus understands that dynamic so He calls His followers to love God more than anybody else, including family. Next in line to love is your family. Our families should never be neglected when following Jesus. There should be a deeper commitment to them as a result of your devotion to God. Disciples of Christ must first pledge their allegiance to Jesus, our commander and chief—the one whose loyalties will never waver in the face of danger. Have you pledged your allegiance to God?

TODAY'S *Commitment* DARE

The fifth commitment dare builds on the previous four. Jesus dares you to love others less than you love God. Jesus dares you to love God more than anyone or anything else. Today, prayerfully resolve to live out God's plan for your life no matter who or what you have to put in second place in order to love God first.

Today's *S. O. A. P.* Study

Scripture:

Luke 14:25-26 Read, Write & Memorize

_____

_____

_____

_____

_____

_____

Observation:

What is God speaking to my heart as I read?

_____

_____

_____

_____

_____

_____

TODAY'S *S. O. A. P.* STUDY

Application:

How does this truth apply to my call to follow Jesus?

_____

_____

_____

_____

_____

_____

Prayer:

In light of what God has shown me, how do I need to pray?

_____

_____

_____

_____

_____

_____

DAY 6
Feed My Sheep

"Too often we underestimate the power of a touch, a smile, a kind word, a listening ear, an honest compliment, or the smallest act of caring, all of which have the potential to turn a life around."

Leo F. Buscaglia

The third time He said to Him, "'Simon son of John, do you love me?" Peter was hurt because Jesus asked Him the third time, "Do you love me?" He said, "Lord, you know all things; you know that I love you." Jesus said, "Feed my sheep"...Then He said to him, "Follow me!"—John 21:17, 19

Jesus trusted Peter, the unqualified fisherman, to lead in His international movement. Jesus' plan was simple. When He shared it with Peter, He did not use a PowerPoint presentation or video introduction. He did repeat Himself three times for emphasis to make sure Peter was paying attention. Are you ready for Jesus' plan to change the world? Care for people. It is simple, yet profound. Was Peter a good candidate for the job? Would you put him on your team? Peter's resume was not impressive at all. If anybody had good reason to doubt Peter's performance, it was Jesus. Peter rebuked Jesus in an attempt to prevent Him from dying on the cross for the sin of the world. Peter denied Jesus three times. Peter lost faith in Jesus as they were both walking on water together. Peter fell asleep when Jesus asked him to pray. From a human standpoint, Peter was the wrong guy for the job, but from God's perspective Peter was perfect for the position.

Most of the military's new recruits join in the same condition Peter joined Jesus' team: unqualified, out of shape, with an unimpressive resume, and a pile of baggage. Like Peter, most recruits possess a degree of zeal and determination to be the best. Once soldiers are committed to following the military's plan, then they become qualified, physically fit, goal driven, and healed from past defeats in order to focus on their future potential. Peter, the only disciple to publicly deny Jesus three times became the only disciple that Jesus commissioned to feed His sheep three times. Peter was ready for action because he was committed to the mission. He had a rocky start, but through his commitment, Jesus trained Peter for combat. You are a perfect candidate for God's international movement. You don't have to get certified to follow Him. All you have to do is commit to caring for people who might not ever be cared for if you do not commit to His mission. Jesus wants to partner with you right where you are in life, in your workplace, in your neighborhood, at your grocery store or in the gym. His mission is for you to care for people in those places.

Caring for people is one of the most significant and meaningful things you can do on earth. For Frank Reed, who was held hostage in a Lebanon cell from 1986 to 1990, the absence of care was worse than anything else. Although he was beaten, made ill, and tormented, Reed felt most the lack of anyone caring. He said in an interview with *Time Magazine*, "Nothing I did mattered to anyone. I began to realize how withering it is to exist without a single expression or caring person around me. I learned one overriding fact: caring is a powerful force. If no one cares, you are truly alone." Care provides the strength to endure. There is a world of people who experience life as Frank Reed did in that cell. They live as if no one cares. If you want to make a difference in the world, care for people. Jesus' plan to reach the world began with His caring for the first twelve disciples. The world, for Jesus, was always that next person who needed care. He cares for you so that you can care for others. The world, for you, is the next person who crosses your path.

TODAY'S *Commitment* DARE

The sixth commitment dare builds on the previous five. Jesus dares you to care for people in such a way that you change their world. Today, prayerfully resolve to live out God's plan for your life no matter who God leads you to care for.

TODAY'S *S. O. A. P.* STUDY

Scripture:

John 21:17, 19 Read, Write & Memorize

_____

_____

_____

_____

_____

_____

Observation:

What is God speaking to my heart as I read?

_____

_____

_____

_____

_____

_____

Today's *S. O. A. P.* Study

Application:

How does this truth apply to my call to follow Jesus?

_____

_____

_____

_____

_____

_____

_____

Prayer:

In light of what God has shown me, how do I need to pray?

_____

_____

_____

_____

_____

_____

_____

DAY 7

Fit for Service

"Unless a definite step is demanded, the call vanishes into thin air, and if men imagine that they can follow Jesus without taking this step, they are deluding themselves like fanatics...Although Peter cannot achieve his own conversion, he can leave his nets."

Dietrich Bonhoeffer

Still another said, "I will follow you, Lord; but first let me go back and say good-by to my family." Jesus replied, "No one who puts his hand to the plow and looks back is fit for service in the Kingdom of God."—Luke 9:61-62

There is nothing more urgent than following Jesus. Apparently, the man who told Jesus he wanted to follow Him had another idea in mind, different from what Jesus says about following Him. Anything other than total commitment will compromise the mission, disqualifying you from being fit for service. If your life was on the line, would you want a police officer to go home first to greet his family before coming to your rescue? The call to follow Christ requires self-denial, a radical first step of sacrifice, so that you are ready to live a life of great sacrifice. Since the world is at stake, Jesus' global mission must consume the life of His followers. A disciple of Christ is first a fulltime servant of God's mission on earth, then responsible to others. Disciples do not schedule their relationship with God and their service for God's mission around jobs, family vacations, or their favorite sports teams' game schedules. They schedule all things around their calling to serve. There is nothing wrong with jobs, family vacations, or having a favorite sports team, unless they cause you to take your hand off the plow and look back, making you unfit for service.

Marines are trained not to look back, but to plow forward no matter the costs. New recruits in the Marines know while at Paris Island that they will be facing hostile fire within weeks. As their preparation intensifies, their attitude must adjust. This turning point in their preparation results in three attitude shifts. This same shifting should take place in the attitudes of disciples.

First, recruits are forced to assume complete responsibility for preparation. They understand that their lives and the lives of others will soon be at risk, so they must be committed to being the best. There is no margin for error. Mistakes cost lives. When urgency is replaced with complacency, disciples entertain the thought of looking back.

Second, the nature of the coming combat forces Marine training to be rigorous. The measure of the training is determined by the expected nature of the challenge and the immeasurable capability of the foes. The level of sacrifice in training will determine the level of sacrifice in combat. Likewise, there is a battle being fought over souls and the enemy is on the prowl. The Bible says in 1 Peter 5:8, "Your enemy the devil prowls around like a roaring lion looking for someone to devour." Those who are fit for service are ready for the enemy's attacks because they are responsible for preparation and committed to rigorous training.

Third, the nature of the recruit's training becomes relevant—tailored to the hardest test he or she will face. The harder and more specific the training, the more equipped for battle you will be. Jesus dares His followers to stand for something larger than life so that they are fit for service. Those who do not commit to His calling will fall for everything, disqualifying themselves from effective service.

TODAY'S *Commitment* DARE

The seventh commitment dare builds on the previous six. Jesus dares you to be fit for service. Jesus dares you not to look back, but to keep your hands on the plow. Today, prayerfully resolve to live out God's plan for your life no matter what you have to leave behind.

TODAY'S *S. O. A. P.* STUDY

Scripture:

Luke 9:61-62 Read, Write & Memorize

_____

_____

_____

_____

_____

_____

Observation:

What is God speaking to my heart as I read?

_____

_____

_____

_____

_____

_____

TODAY'S *S. O. A. P.* STUDY

Application:

How does this truth apply to my call to follow Jesus?

_____

_____

_____

_____

_____

_____

Prayer:

In light of what God has shown me, how do I need to pray?

_____

_____

_____

_____

_____

_____

DAY 8

Blessed

*"The Lord Jesus puts His finger on every inch of
my existence and says 'Mine; Mine; Mine.'"*

Abraham Kuyper

*Now when He saw the crowds, He went up on a mountainside and sat
down. His disciples came to Him, and He began to teach them saying:
"Blessed are the poor in spirit, for theirs is the kingdom of heaven."*
—*Matthew 5:1-3*

Character is a community issue. Your character is developed best in
community. The way people live in front of you influences the way you
live in front of others. The closer you are to other followers of Christ
that are striving to live a life marked with a godly character, the more
your character will develop. If you live life disconnected from a Christ-
centered community, your character will be undeveloped and you will
not be as effective in God's mission as you could.

Jesus introduced His most popular sermon with God's "Bucket
List" of character traits otherwise known as the "Be-Attitudes." A
bucket list is a list of things to accomplish before you kick the bucket—
die. Most people fill their bucket list with things to do, but God's bucket
list for His people contains things to be. God is more interested in who
you are than what you do. God has prepared for His followers a path in
life full of good works. If you lack character, then you will miss opportunities to do good works that He has prepared for you to accomplish.
For example, if you are a greedy person, then you will miss opportunities to be generous. If you are a lustful person, then you will miss opportunities to love. Jesus never compromised His character regardless of
who provoked Him or what happened. Even on the cross when He was
abused, His character prevailed with meekness, one of the beatitudes.
The life He was killed for was a life marked by godly character.

Few people actually live a life worth dying for, a life marked with
godly character, as Jesus did. There was one girl who did. Her name was

Perpetua. She was a young woman of noble birth. She was twenty-two, a wife, a mother of a young son, and a Christian. In the city of Carthage in North Africa on March 7, 203 she was put to death for her religious convictions. She was given countless opportunities to lie, but because her character would not allow her, she could not do anything but tell the truth. When the authorities would ask her to denounce her faith in Christ, all she had to do was cross her fingers and say a little lie. But to her, it was impossible because she was a person of godly character who told the truth. Perpetua's father, a pagan, often came to the prison, even with her son in his arms, to plead with her to deny Christ in order to save her life.

One day Perpetua wrote, "When I was in the hands of the persecutors, my father in his tender solicitude tried hard to keep me from the faith. 'My father,' I said, 'you see this pitcher. Can we call it by any other name than what it is?' 'No,' he said. 'Nor can I,' I said, 'call myself by any other name than that of Christian.'" The character of a disciple is not to be compromised, even in the face of death. Your character sets you apart from unbelievers. It is the weapon God equipped every disciple with to bring change in their community. A disciple of Christ is called to be a person of godly character. You are fully approved by God when you take the path in life marked by godly character. To be blessed by God is more than happiness; it is to be completely satisfied in who you are. The best way to experience the blessing of God is to live a godly life marked by godly character. Fulfilling His mission on earth requires character. Are you living the blessed life—a life of character?

TODAY'S *Character* DARE

The foundation for the transformation of your character is sacrifice. Living a life marked with great sacrifice calls for an extreme alteration of your character. Today, prayerfully resolve to live a life marked with godly character no matter who challenges you to be anything other than a pitcher!

TODAY'S *S. O. A. P.* STUDY

Scripture:

Matthew 5:1-3 Read, Write & Memorize

_____

_____

_____

_____

_____

_____

Observation:

What is God speaking to my heart as I read?

_____

_____

_____

_____

_____

_____

TODAY'S *S. O. A. P.* STUDY

Application:

How does this truth apply to my call to follow Jesus?

_____

_____

_____

_____

_____

_____

Prayer:

In light of what God has shown me, how do I need to pray?

_____

_____

_____

_____

_____

_____

DAY 9

Poor in Spirit

"Character is what you have left when you've lost everything you can lose."

Evan Esar

Now when He saw the crowds, He went up on a mountainside and sat down. His disciples came to him, and He began to teach them saying: "Blessed are the poor in spirit, for theirs is the kingdom of heaven."
—Matthew 5:1-3

God's people should be the most humble people on the planet. When Jesus' audience heard the phrase "poor in spirit," they would immediately think back to the exile. In the days when Babylon was a superpower, the people of Israel thought of themselves as invincible. The temple was a point of pride for them. They could not imagine anyone destroying the place where the presence of God dwelled. This led them to become prideful as a community. Their lives became full of idolatry. They worshipped other pagan gods. Through all their disobedience, God was patient with them. He warned them to stop countless times, but they persisted to rebel against Him. They thought He would never judge them, but they were wrong. God used the pagan nation of Babylon to judge the Israelites for their sin. Everything, including the temple, was destroyed; many people were killed and those who were not killed were exiled to Babylon. This was one of the lowest moments in Israel's history. The community of Israel was completely broken.

Before the exile, Israel depended on the temple to worship God. They thought that as long as they went through the motions at the temple, making the required offerings, God would overlook their sin. The exile exposed their pride. If they were going to live for God then they had to acknowledge their brokenness. They were physically destitute and had nowhere else to turn but to God. They realized the first step to wholeness was humility. They were not to be dependent on their own efforts anymore but solely on God. Israel is our spiritual ancestor. Like the Jewish people who followed Israel's exile, we are also spiritually exiled. We are broken people without God, just as they were. Wholeness is the result of living a life marked with godly character. We need God more than we need anything else in life. Nothing trumps our need for God, no amount of money could be earned or position could be achieved that excludes anyone from complete dependence on God.

In God's economy, less is more; bigger is not better. Humility says, "I must give myself a personal demotion to receive God's promotion." James 4:10 says it like this: "Humble yourselves before the Lord, and He will lift you up." The more brokenness you bring to God the more wholeness you can experience. The "poor in spirit" are those who know they are spiritually bankrupt. They know they have nothing to offer God but their brokenness. Brokenness before God is the antidote for pride before the world. The most broken people are the most humble people. The most effective disciples in God's army are humble disciples, because the better we understand that we have nothing to offer God, the more you have to offer people. There is nothing you can do to make yourself right before God except to humble yourself before God in brokenness. It takes a humble person to admit he or she is spiritually bankrupt and to live this way in front of others.

TODAY'S *Character* DARE

Living as "poor in spirit" is not popular in today's culture that prides itself of being "rich in spirit." God designed His army of disciples to change the world by relying only on Him. Today, prayerfully consider living completely dependent on God.

TODAY'S *S.O.A.P.* STUDY

Scripture:

Matthew 5:1-3 Read, Write & Memorize

_____

_____

_____

_____

_____

_____

Observation:

What is God speaking to my heart as I read?

_____

_____

_____

_____

_____

_____

TODAY'S *S. O. A. P.* STUDY

Application:

How does this truth apply to my call to follow Jesus?

_____

_____

_____

_____

_____

_____

Prayer:

In light of what God has shown me, how do I need to pray?

_____

_____

_____

_____

_____

_____

DAY 10

Kingdom of Heaven

"The church... is not meant to call men and women out of the world into a safe religious enclave but to call them out in order to send them back as agents of God's kingship."

Lesslie Newbigin

Now when He saw the crowds, He went up on a mountainside and sat down. His disciples came to him, and He began to teach them saying: "Blessed are the poor in spirit, for theirs is the kingdom of heaven."
—*Matthew 5:1-3*

God's people should be the most kingdom-minded people on the planet. Jesus is a master at casting inspiring vision, a vision worth dying for. In Matthew 5:3, Jesus shared His vision for the "Kingdom of Heaven." Using present tense language, Jesus proclaimed that the Kingdom is now. Jesus' life and ministry on earth ushered in the Kingdom of Heaven also known as the "Kingdom of God." God's Kingdom has already started. Wherever God's people are, the power of God's Kingdom is present and active. The Kingdom of God is the rule and reign of God on earth. Stanley Horton writes, It's "the sphere of God's rule." God rules and reigns in the hearts of those who partner with His worldwide mission. He reigns over us by love, not by force and control. The Kingdom flips the world right-side-up. "The Kingdom of God has none of the usual characteristics of an earthly kingdom. In the kingdom [of God] all earthly values are reversed. The first shall be last, and the last shall be first. The greatest people in the kingdom shall be servants" (See followingjesus.org/vision/traditional_interpretations.htm).

The Kingdom of God is transformational. It has the power to completely restore the world to the way it was before sin, evil, brokenness and death, the way it will be when God restores all things in the future. God promises that those who are part of His kingdom while on earth will experience its transformational power. Jesus' vision for the

Kingdom of God is freedom from oppressive earthly systems and healing from human brokenness and weakness. The power of the Kingdom of God is seen in the King's people. The King's people who live like the King create a new world order. This new world order began with Jesus, but "exists side by side with the old order of Satan. Someday God's new order will fill the earth. Until that day, we are called to live out God's new order—of equality, humility, servanthood, compassion, forgiveness, nonviolence, and sharing—in the midst of the old" (See followingjesus.org/vision/vision_jesus.htm).

The Kingdom of God is revolutionary. In God's strategy to transform the world, He includes the transformation of your character. God's people should have the finest character on the planet. If God's Kingdom is going to change the world for the better, the world must experience a revolution of godly character by the King's people. The character of our King is represented by the character of the King's people. Your character ushers in God's kingdom in your work place, your neighborhood, your home front, or wherever you are. You can bring restoration to the people who are hurting, broken, and dying by living out the character of God's kingdom in front of them. His future promises then become a present reality for them. If you want to change the world, it includes changing your character. All it takes is one person to undergo a radical character shift to start a revolution.

TODAY'S *Character* DARE

God dares you to accept His character challenge. God promises to restore the world as you represent a life marked by godly character. Today, prayerfully resolve to usher in God's kingdom wherever you go, no matter how much your character must change.

TODAY'S *S. O. A. P.* STUDY

Scripture:

Matthew 5:1-3 Read, Write & Memorize

_____

_____

_____

_____

_____

_____

Observation:

What is God speaking to my heart as I read?

_____

_____

_____

_____

_____

_____

TODAY'S *S.O.A.P.* STUDY

Application:

How does this truth apply to my call to follow Jesus?

_____

_____

_____

_____

_____

_____

_____

Prayer:

In light of what God has shown me, how do I need to pray?

_____

_____

_____

_____

_____

_____

_____

DAY 11

Comfort

"Learn from yesterday, live for today, hope for tomorrow."
Albert Einstein

"Blessed are those who mourn, for they will be comforted."—Matthew 5:4

God's people should be the most hopeful people on the planet. There is hope even in the midst of pain. The nation of Israel was hopeless after the exile. As a community, they sinned against God, and as a community, they were judged by God. They lost everything in which they prided themselves. The temple was completely demolished, their land was destroyed, and many people were killed. They paid the consequences for their sin, leading them into painful regret for their actions. But in the midst of great pain, there is great hope. In the midst of their sin, the prophet Isaiah had a similar message to Jesus. He said, "The Spirit of the Sovereign LORD is on me because the LORD has anointed me…to proclaim the year of the LORD's favor and the day of vengeance of our God, to comfort all who mourn…" (Isaiah 61:1-2). Jesus' promise of comfort originated with the prophet Isaiah, but was fulfilled in His ministry. Jesus promises you that even in the midst of pain, whether it is self-caused or from an outside source, there is comfort. It is a guarantee. It might not be on your timetable, or how you expect it, but in the end God will heal our brokenness and relieve our pain.

There is hope even in hopeless places. There is comfort even in painful situations. Not many people feel more pain than Mrs. Washington. Her daughter was killed by a man named Ron Flowers, who maintained his innocence for 15 years. Mrs. Washington was outraged towards him, writing letters to the parole board every time he was up for parole. Then Ron joined the Sycamore Tree project, a Prison Fellowship program that helps offenders to confess Christ and make restitution to their victims, and for the first time he admitted his crime and prayed that his victim's family would forgive him. At his Sycamore Tree Project graduation ceremony, as he approached for his certificate for completing 18 months, Mrs. Washington rose from her seat among the many visitors. She hurried to the front, wrapped her arms around him, and declared to everyone present, "This young man is my adopted son." The place was electrified. According to Chuck Colson, hardened criminals and tough corrections officials had tears in their eyes, for they knew that this young man was behind bars for the murder of Mrs. Washington's daughter.

There is hope in the most painful circumstances. Accepting responsibility for his fault led to Ron's freedom from his personal guilt. Mrs. Washington then was able to radically forgive Ron, finding freedom from her unrepentant heart for him. Ron's sphere of influence was affected by the sin, loss, and pain of one person, yet it was healed by the repentance of one person. Those who follow Christ comfort those who mourn loss. They become empathetic to the pain resulting form their loss, seeking to relieve it at all costs. The community-at-large can be transformed by the character of one person. The disciple who is able to be hopeful in the midst of pain will comfort the community. When Ron Flowers was released after Mrs. Washington pleaded with the parole board on his behalf, she gave him a significant amount of money, enough to get a new start in life. How are you showing hope in hopeless situations? Don't live another day without hope.

TODAY'S *Character* DARE

God dares you to be hopeful in times of loss so that you can comfort others in times of pain. Today, prayerfully resolve to be hopeful no matter how severe the loss or who is responsible. Remember, God uses your character to help restore the world.

TODAY'S *S. O. A. P.* STUDY

Scripture:

Matthew 5:4 Read, Write & Memorize

_____

_____

_____

_____

_____

_____

Observation:

What is God speaking to my heart as I read?

_____

_____

_____

_____

_____

_____

Today's *S. O. A. P.* Study

Application:

How does this truth apply to my call to follow Jesus?

_____

_____

_____

_____

_____

_____

Prayer:

In light of what God has shown me, how do I need to pray?

_____

_____

_____

_____

_____

_____

DAY 12

Meek

"People who are meek commit all their business, their problems and their relationships, their fears, their frustrations and their health to God in the firm conviction that God is able and willing to sustain, guide and protect them."

Charmaine Braatvedt

"Blessed are the meek, for they will inherit the earth."—Matthew 5:5

God's people should be the most balanced people on the planet. In God's Kingdom, meekness is not a weakness but rather shows strength under control. A meek person in the Greek sense of the term was controlled and balanced, getting angry at the right things and at the right time. A meek person, for example, would get angry of injustice in the world, according to Haddon W. Robinson, former interim President at Gordon-Conwell Theological Seminary.

There was a story about a young soldier in the Peloponnesian Wars who wrote to his fiancée about a gift he had for her. The gift was a white stallion, and he described it as the most magnificent animal he had ever seen. He said, "It responds obediently to the slightest command. He allows his master to direct him to his full potential." And then he wrote, "He is a meek horse." The stallion was an animal with great spirit, but that spirit was submissive to the rider. Meekness has the sense of great strength, like a stallion that is under control.

The nation of Israel learned firsthand how being meek results in the inheritance of land. Israel lost its land at the hands of the ancient world's superpower. The Babylonian kings conquered the land of Israel through force. The process in which God would restore the land to them was not through force but through the Israelites' meekness as they trusted God for Him to act on their behalf. The last people in the world who should have received an inheritance were the Israelites after the exile, especially since they were not militarily strong. However, God restored them despite their weaknesses and wickedness. He reconquered their land without resorting to warfare. They were promised an inheritance of land without exercising brute force, something the superpowers of the day could not imagine. The only conceivable way to inherit land was to take it by force from others. The people of God do not have to flex their muscles, but through patience, will receive their inheritance by maintaining self-control.

Jesus modeled meekness on the cross. He could have called 10,000 angels to wipe out the people who were insulting him, spitting on him, and beating Him senseless. Instead of fighting fire with fire, He exercised strength under control. He was balanced. He trusted God and did not force His inheritance, even though He was entitled to it. He gave up His right to be right. Are you forcing your inheritance? Have you given up your right to be right? Or do you live as if you are entitled to everything? Jesus' disciples are called to be balanced in the midst of a competitive culture. Meek people do not rush God into action, nor do they do anything to get ahead of God. The meek wait for God to give them their inheritance as they exercise strength under control.

TODAY'S *Character* DARE

God dares you to be balanced, not exercising your right to be right. Meek people understand they are not entitled to their inheritance until God gives it to them. Today, prayerfully resolve to be meek no matter how long you have to wait for your inheritance.

TODAY'S *S. O. A. P.* STUDY

Scripture:

Matthew 5:5 Read, Write & Memorize

_____

_____

_____

_____

_____

_____

Observation:

What is God speaking to my heart as I read?

_____

_____

_____

_____

_____

TODAY'S *S.O.A.P.* STUDY

Application:

How does this truth apply to my call to follow Jesus?

_____

_____

_____

_____

_____

_____

Prayer:

In light of what God has shown me, how do I need to pray?

_____

_____

_____

_____

_____

_____

DAY 13

Righteous

*"Loving what is right is different from hating
what is wrong and feeling right about it."*

Roy Masters

*"Blessed are those who hunger and thirst for righteousness, for they will
be filled."*—Matthew 5:6

God's people should be the most mature people on the planet.
Your maturity as a disciple results from your commitment to live for
the fulfillment of God's plans and purposes on earth. What you hunger
and thirst for in life will determine your righteousness. Those who pursue righteousness will mature, but those who go off in the wrong directions will become immature, stuck in the rut of self-righteousness. To
be righteous is to live your life in line with God's plans and purposes
on earth. Those who live for God's righteousness on earth will change
the world, one relationship at a time. Those who live for self-
righteousness will expect the world to change for them. Godly character is developed when disciples of Christ hunger and thirst for those
things that concern God. The righteousness of God is a future promise
that has results in the present. One day God will completely restore all
brokenness in every direction: God, self, others, and the world. A day is
coming when relational dysfunction will be healed in all directions, but
until then only some brokenness will be made whole and not all relationships will be functional.

The mission of God's people is to restore the world. You are
God's agent of change. You were created to set things right in your

world as God intended. Your life will bring justice to the oppressed, healing to the broken hearted, freedom to the addicted, love to the outcast, and truth to the deceived. You are God's representative in your workplace, neighborhood, or local grocery store. You are called by God to make things right in a world that has gone off in the wrong direction. God calls us to care about the things He cares about like poverty, hunger, morality, politics, and religion. Disciples whose godly character leads them in the direction of making righteous change in their world will make an eternal difference.

The righteousness of God is counter-cultural. God calls His followers to selflessness; not to a selfish, self-reliant, or self-absorbed life. If we are going to make a difference in the world, then we have to be different from the world. God calls us to live *in the world*, not to be *of the world*. We must reflect His character, which is different from everyone else's. There is no room for compromise, only commitment. His plan to restore the world is not open for suggestions, only obedience. Living for God's righteousness does not protect your future; it might complicate it. God promises that you will be fully approved by Him when you live to set things right. There is nothing more satisfying in life than to be part of God's mission on earth as His righteousness renews, restores, and reconciles culture.

TODAY'S *Character* DARE

God dares you to set things right in all directions: God, self, others, and the world. Today, prayerfully consider pursuing righteousness above all else no matter how strong the temptation to hunger and thirst for other things is.

Today's *S. O. A. P.* Study

Scripture:

Matthew 5:6 Read, Write & Memorize

_____

_____

_____

_____

_____

_____

Observation:

What is God speaking to my heart as I read?

_____

_____

_____

_____

_____

TODAY'S *S.O.A.P.* STUDY

Application:

How does this truth apply to my call to follow Jesus?

_____

_____

_____

_____

_____

_____

Prayer:

In light of what God has shown me, how do I need to pray?

_____

_____

_____

_____

_____

_____

_____

DAY 14

Satisfied

"I have never met a soul who has set out to satisfy the Lord and has not been satisfied himself."

Watchman Nee

"Blessed are those who hunger and thirst for righteousness, for they will be filled."—Matthew 5:6

God's people should be the most satisfied people on the planet; but we tend to be just as unsatisfied as anybody else. We live in a "monster of more" culture where bigger is better and the latest is the greatest. But at the end of the day, it is never enough. The larger and better television screens become, the more unsatisfied we become with ours. This principle works in all areas of life. The more advanced our culture becomes, the less satisfied people are. The problem is not with our hunger and thirst for more, but with what we hunger and thirst for. What we are hungry and thirsty for in life will determine if we will be satisfied or not. The only thing that can eternally satisfy the human hunger for more is to live your life in line with God's mission on earth.

There is nothing in life that satisfies our longing for more like working at changing and restoring the culture. Jesus calls His followers to be hungry and thirsty for cultural renewal. Every follower of Christ is called to be salt and light in the world. Salt makes things grow. Light makes things more visible. Salt produces the flourishing of human life. Light brings out the best in human life. Both of them are influencing agents that promote change. As a disciple of Christ with godly character, you are a catalyst of change and an example of human goodness. The amount of influence you have in culture is only as strong as the amount of commitment you make to living a life marked by godly character. If you are hungry and thirsty for righteousness, then you will be satisfied by being salt and light. But if you are more hungry and thirsty for TVs, DVDs and MP3s, then you will not renew the culture, but become a victim of cultural decay. You will starve for the wrong things, never finding fulfillment in life. God will satisfy you, if you are hungry and thirsty for God's worldwide mission on the earth.

The only thing that eternally satisfies our internal hunger and thirst for more in life is living righteously. There is no satisfaction that fulfills like living to restore harmony in all directions. Our culture is a mission field. Your mission is to renew your home front, your neighborhood, your workplace, and your community. When you embody godly character, you will prevent cultural decay from taking root and destroying everything around you. The plan to renew the culture is not to turn your back from it or to not participate in it, but to be present. Your presence in culture calls for you to be culturally discerning,—the ability to reflectively engage culture through a biblical lens. The presence of a disciple in culture who commits to living for God's righteousness, not self-righteousness, will renew, restore, and reconcile relationships in all directions: God, self, others, and the world. Cultural renewal satisfies our hunger and thirst for more of God and for His Kingdom to come on earth.

TODAY'S *Character* DARE

God dares you to search for satisfaction in His righteousness not satisfaction in worldly pleasures. Today, prayerfully resolve to only be satisfied by doing things that concern God's plans and purposes on earth.

Today's *S. O. A. P.* Study

Scripture:

Matthew 5:6 Read, Write & Memorize

_____

_____

_____

_____

_____

_____

Observation:

What is God speaking to my heart as I read?

_____

_____

_____

_____

_____

_____

TODAY'S *S.O.A.P.* STUDY

Application:

How does this truth apply to my call to follow Jesus?

_____

_____

_____

_____

_____

_____

_____

Prayer:

In light of what God has shown me, how do I need to pray?

_____

_____

_____

_____

_____

_____

_____

DAY 15
Merciful

"A...mercy, which yields to danger will be...merciful only on conditions. Pilate was merciful till it became risky."

C.S. Lewis

"Blessed are the merciful, for they will be shown mercy."—Matthew. 5:7

God's people should be the most merciful people on the planet. Since we live in a cutthroat culture with people who are looking to kick you when you're down, those who show mercy will make a world of difference. The only way to change the heartless tune of the culture is to be merciful at all times, no matter what. Even if your neighbor severely wrongs you or your family, show them mercy. Only those who show mercy will receive mercy (James 2:13). Not responding first with mercy shows the world God's mercy has not fully impacted your life. Having mercy means showing compassion, not just feeling compassion. According to John MacArthur, it refers to the ability to get inside someone else's skin until you think their thoughts, feel their emotions, understand their pain, and then seek to relieve it. Mercy is empathy, not just sympathy. Showing sympathy is like throwing a life jacket to someone who is drowning, but being empathetic and merciful is like jumping in headfirst to save the person. There is a world full of people out there who are drowning. They need someone who is willing to enter into their pain and help them to heal from their misery.

Jesus always dove headfirst into people's pain. He cared so much for people that the Bible records Jesus crying (John 11:35). "Jesus wept," when Lazarus died. The smallest Bible verse speaks one of the greatest truths about Jesus: He was a person of mercy. God expects His followers to be known for showing mercy. Jesus changed the world one act of mercy at a time. His itinerant ministry was marked by random acts of mercy. He became extremely popular for showing mercy. Almost everywhere He went, people would seek Him out. The two blind men, the Samaritan woman, and the father of a demon-possessed son all described Jesus as one who was able to show them mercy. People were attracted to Him because they knew He genuinely cared about their pain. Jesus was famous for entering into the pain of others. What are you famous for—entering in and relieving the pain of others or ignoring and neglecting the pain of others?

Fiorello LaGuardia was the mayor of New York City from 1934 to 1945. He was said to have shown up at a night court in the poorest ward of the city in 1935 during the depression. He dismissed the judge for the evening and took over the bench. One case he heard involved an elderly woman who was caught stealing bread to feed her grandchildren. LaGuardia said, "I've got to punish you. $10 or 10 days in jail." As he spoke, he threw $10 into his hat. He then fined everyone in the courtroom 50 cents for living in a city "where a person has to steal bread so her grandchildren can eat." The hat was passed around, and the woman left the courtroom with her fine paid and an additional $47.50. What do people leave your presence with? Do they leave with mercy, or do they leave in pain? If people know they are safe around you and their failures are not going to be rubbed in, then they will follow you wherever you lead them.

TODAY'S *Character* DARE

God dares you to be generous with mercy, not withholding it from those who are in pain. The greatest act of mercy took place on the cross when Jesus entered into the pain of the world. He does not expect you to show the entire world mercy, but to show mercy to the next person in pain. Today, prayerfully resolve to follow in Jesus' footsteps by living a life marked by generous acts of mercy.

Today's *S.O.A.P.* Study

Scripture:

Matthew 5:7 Read, Write & Memorize

_____

_____

_____

_____

_____

Observation:

What is God speaking to my heart as I read?

_____

_____

_____

_____

_____

TODAY'S *S. O. A. P.* STUDY

Application:

How does this truth apply to my call to follow Jesus?

_____

_____

_____

_____

_____

_____

Prayer:

In light of what God has shown me, how do I need to pray?

_____

_____

_____

_____

_____

_____

DAY 16
Pure

*"If you can't trust the messenger, you can't trust
the message."*
Anonymous Author

"Blessed are the pure in heart, for they will see God."—Matthew 5:8

God's people should be the most pure people on the planet. God's
global mission advances as His disciples fight for godly purity. Carl
Bauman said, "Until you have proven your integrity no one will follow
you anywhere." Purity of heart (integrity) validates your ministry. You
should live your life under a microscope for all to see. There should not
be any skeletons in your closet as you follow Christ. He paid the price
on the cross for you to keep your closet open. If you attempt to follow
Christ with a closet full of sin, then you are not headed in the right direction. God does not call us to be perfect, but to always be moving in
the right direction.

The people with the most integrity are the people with the most accountability. As Bob Rhoden says, accountability is simply telling the necessary people the necessary information before it is necessary. It is not
sharing about your skeletons when they come out of your closet to haunt
you. Accountability prevents skeletons from piling up and overloading
the closet of your life. The by-product of accountability is integrity.

People with integrity have clear focus in life. Bobby Jones is considered one of the history's greatest golfers. He won thirteen majors before
he retired at the age of twenty-eight. He was the first player to win four
majors in one year! But even more than his winning record on the golf
course, Bobby Jones is famous for a one-shot penalty at the 1925 U.S.

Open. According to Mark Batterson, Jones inadvertently touched his golf ball and assessed himself a one stroke penalty, even though no one saw him touch the ball: not the tournament official and not his playing partner. Neither of them believed he actually touched the ball. Bobby Jones could have easily justified not taking the penalty. No one saw it. It didn't affect anything. The tournament official said, "Well, Bobby, it is up to you. Do you believe you touched the ball?" To which Bobby responded, "I know that I did." And he assessed himself a one-stroke penalty. Bobby Jones lost the 1925 U.S. Open by one stroke. When reporters tried to interview him about the self-imposed penalty, Bobby Jones forbade them from writing about it. He said it would be inappropriate because there was nothing extraordinary about playing by the rules. Bobby Jones could have compromised his integrity and won the match, but he chose to lose the match and keep his integrity. He wasn't willing to compromise one stroke. What if we weren't willing to compromise one stroke?

The result of purity of heart is the ability to see God. No one will see God personally on this side of eternity, but His presence lives in His followers. The power of God's rule and reign started by Jesus purifies us from the inside out. Those who are pure in heart have an internal integrity that manifests itself in how they live. Your behavior in life follows your heart. Only a pure heart will produce good fruit. The fruit of your heart will show people God. They will not see Him physically, but will see His character through your actions. Show the world a pure heart, and they will see a pure God who is worth following.

TODAY'S *Character* DARE

God dares you to be a person of integrity. If God does not rule your heart, then He will not rule your life. Today, prayerfully resolve to strive for purity in all areas of life.

TODAY'S *S. O. A. P.* STUDY

Scripture:

Matthew 5:8 Read, Write & Memorize

_____

_____

_____

_____

_____

_____

Observation:

What is God speaking to my heart as I read?

_____

_____

_____

_____

_____

_____

TODAY'S *S.O.A.P.* STUDY

Application:

How does this truth apply to my call to follow Jesus?

_____

_____

_____

_____

_____

_____

Prayer:

In light of what God has shown me, how do I need to pray?

_____

_____

_____

_____

_____

_____

DAY 17

Peacemaker

"You can't have the peace of God until you know the God of Peace."

Gerry A. Bass

"Blessed are the peacemakers, for they will be called sons of God."
—*Matthew 5:9*

God's people should be the most peaceful people on the planet. Those who work for peace in God's international movement restore order in all directions: self, God, others, and the world. There is no relationship in which you should not fight for peace. There is no person beyond restoration. To better understand Jesus' words about peace, we must first understand the Hebrew word for peace: *shalom*. According to William Holladay, *shalom* means "wholeness, intact; prosperity, peace; well-being." The verb form means, "To be completed, to be healthy, and to keep peace." It is not just the absence of war, although that is part of what *shalom* means. *Shalom* also means all that is good for you in life. It means complete restoration. The restoration of all things will be experienced only partially as we fight for peace; but at the end of time our restoration will be complete. Until then, God's people are responsible for bringing some of that *shalom* to their home front, workplace, neighborhood, and community.

Peacemaking is part of God's character. He is frequently referred to as the "God of Peace" (Romans 15:33, 2 Cor. 13:11, Philippians 4:9). God's people are called to be peacemakers, not prizefighters—those who do not fight for peace at all costs. The character of God is to be reflected in the character of God's people. If your life is not marked by peace, then you will be a prizefighter, not peacemaker. If peace is a characteristic of who you are, then you will fight for peace at all costs.

Fighting for peace does not mean never having conflict. Peacemakers confront people lovingly. Loving confrontation is active peacemaking, not passive peacefaking. Not restoring the order or functionality in a relationship is faking peace. God is the master of loving confrontation. He did not leave us in our sin, but confronted it lovingly. He did not withdraw from conflict, but confronted it peacefully. He loved the world enough to bring peace on earth by sending His son to die on the cross for our sin, disorders, problems, and diseases.

Peacemaking is love in action. You have not loved someone until you have made peace with him or her. Leaving conflict unresolved is not showing love (Mark 12:31). Peacemakers resolve conflict at all cost. There is spiritual conflict between God and people. As an agent of peace, you are called to bridge that gap by loving people into a relationship with God. You might be the only disciple of Christ many unbelievers encounter in their lifetime, and if you are not a person of peace, then you might miss the opportunity to confront their spiritual conflicts.

As Sam Schutz has said, God's people are called to wage war for peace. If there are families around you who are broken, then it's going to take you to fight for peace on their behalf. If they see someone else fighting for peace, then it will inspire them to do the same. If there are any relationships in your sphere of influence headed in the wrong direction, then you must fight for peace on their behalf. If there are any people you know out of control in their personal life, then fight for peace on their behalf. Those who fight for peace seek to resolve conflict, not sweep it under the rug. They seek to restore wholeness in people's lives, not ignoring their brokenness. Are you a peacemaker or prizefighter?

TODAY'S *Character* DARE

God dares you to fight for peace at all cost. Today, prayerfully resolve to confront people lovingly and seek to reconcile relationships in all directions.

TODAY'S *S.O.A.P.* STUDY

Scripture:

Matthew 5:9 Read, Write & Memorize

_____

_____

_____

_____

_____

_____

Observation:

What is God speaking to my heart as I read?

_____

_____

_____

_____

_____

_____

_____

TODAY'S *S. O. A. P.* STUDY

Application:

How does this truth apply to my call to follow Jesus?

_____

_____

_____

_____

_____

_____

Prayer:

In light of what God has shown me, how do I need to pray?

_____

_____

_____

_____

_____

_____

DAY 18

Children of God

"Yet to all who received him [Jesus Christ]...he gave the right to become children of God."

The Apostle John

"Blessed are the peacemakers, for they will be called sons of God."
—*Matthew 5:9*

God's people are part of His family. Peacemakers are authentic members of God's family. Peacemaking is a significant part of God's family business. Family members share responsibilities. Peacemaking, not prizefighting or peacefaking, is a priority in the family of God. God has not brought peace into your life for you to hide it from others. God has redeemed your life in order to restore others and bring peace to them. Peacemaking calls us to fall forward towards conflict, not to fall back away from it. The family of God grows through proactive, loving confrontation but shrinks through passive, unresolved conflict. The Kingdom of God advances when the King's family members adopt the posture of peacemaking, not the causal gesture of peacefaking.

God's people should be the best at handling conflict on the planet. God is the master of conflict resolution. It is part of His DNA, which makes it part of His children's spiritual DNA. Conflict is normal and healthy in families. There was and still is conflict between humanity and God. The reason for the conflict was the wickedness of sinful man, but the reason for reconciliation is the righteousness of Jesus. He died to resolve the conflict between humanity and God. His life, death, and resurrection restored mankind to its original purposes and plan before Adam and Eve's first sin. At that time, there was no conflict between God and humanity, only perfect harmony; no division between people, only perfect unity; no personal internal struggles, only complete order.

They experienced heaven on earth in all directions: God, self, others, and the world.

This is the only beatitude that tells you others will notice you because of it, "You will be called the sons of God." People will either identify you as a peacemaker or prizefighter. Peacemakers resolve conflict at all costs for the right reasons. Prizefighters provoke unnecessary conflict and fail to make resolutions. All of us have a reputation of peacemaking or prizefighting. If you want to know what yours is, ask the people closest to you—usually the people closest to you see you at your best and worst. Only a person who has a conviction of making peace will fight for order in their homes, workplaces, neighbors, and communities.

Today heaven on earth results from promoting peace in all directions. God has given His family tall marching orders. God commands His family members to love their neighbors but also to love their enemies. Everyone you meet falls on that spectrum. If you are married, then your spouse is your closest neighbor, even if you think they are your worst enemy! Since they are in closest proximity to you, they should be loved the most. God expects us to love our enemies as He loved us: sacrificially, unconditionally, and patiently. The love God commands is the kind of love you show those who are in your biological family. It is a covenant love. It is a kinship love, a love that transcends boundaries, races, ethnicities, and cultures. There is a spiritual connection to those in the family of God that transcends biological relations. Love all people sacrificially, because you will never know who God will call to be His child as a result of rubbing shoulders with you.

TODAY'S *Character* DARE

God dares you to love people into a relationship with God. Today, prayerfully resolve to love all people as members of your family.

TODAY'S *S. O. A. P.* STUDY

Scripture:

Matthew 5:9 Read, Write & Memorize

_____

_____

_____

_____

_____

_____

Observation:

What is God speaking to my heart as I read?

_____

_____

_____

_____

_____

_____

TODAY'S *S. O. A. P.* STUDY

Application:

How does this truth apply to my call to follow Jesus?

_____

_____

_____

_____

_____

Prayer:

In light of what God has shown me, how do I need to pray?

_____

_____

_____

_____

_____

DAY 19

Persecution

*"Virtue is persecuted more by the wicked
than it is loved by the good."*

Anonymous Author

*"Blessed are those who are persecuted because of righteousness, for theirs is
the kingdom of heaven."—Matthew 5:10*

God's people should be the most persecuted people on the planet. Jesus was persecuted to the point of death because He did what was right. Jesus embodied the character of God. He had no other choice but to behave based on His character. His character moved Him to reform the Jewish religious system, a system that focused on rules, not on relationship with God. He was persecuted for it because He resolved to live a life marked with godly character, even if it cost Him His life. Jesus was persecuted because He was not ashamed or fearful of living out His character in front of others. His character was part of everything He did and part of everything He was persecuted for.

Godly character will be persecuted by the ungodly. It is a fact. Living a life marked by godly character is radically different than the character of today's culture, but it is also the very strategy of God for bringing restoration in all directions: God, self, others, and the world. The word *persecute* means "to pursue." People will sometimes go out of their way to pursue you just so they can make your life miserable. But we are blessed if we are persecuted for righteousness. Persecution is sometimes a by-product of living a life marked with godly character. It will not only solidify your faith in God, but will shake the unbelieving persecutor's lack of faith. The soldier who dies in battle fighting for his country not only compels others to fight harder, but frightens his enemy, possibly causing him to surrender. Jesus died in battle. His followers must fight harder, never surrendering but leading others to surrender as they live out their godly character regardless of whether or not they are persecuted for it in the battlefield of life. If we're not persecuted every once in a while, then we're probably not making our Christianity visible. Our character should show our beliefs. If we're living the kind of life Jesus died for then people should respond to us either with curiosity, wanting to know more or with persecution, wanting to know less.

Persecution is not punishment. When we are punished, we get what we deserve. Punishment is what so-called "just" people give to those deemed evil. Persecution is what evil people give to those who are good. According to Daniel McNaughton, in God's kingdom, He blesses His followers when evil people go out of their way to hurt them because they did the right thing. There is purpose in persecution. God does not waste any pain experienced through persecution. God's kingdom advances through the persecution of His followers. When people insult you or criticize your character for following in the footsteps of Jesus, His kingdom benefits. It might not make sense in the moment. It might even hurt, but your resolve speaks volumes to the person doing the persecuting.

Question your walk with God, when you live in such a way that no one ever even looks at you the wrong way for following Jesus. Sometimes the most blessed moments of your life will be the most painful. Your pain will ultimately subside, but your legacy will live forever in the Kingdom of Heaven. You only have one life to live. Make it count for Christ. What do people think of Jesus when they see your life? Is Jesus Lord, or is he a liar and lunatic?

TODAY'S *Character* DARE

God dares you to endure persecution. Today, prayerfully resolve to live unashamedly and fearlessly a life marked with godly character no matter how much persecution you endure.

TODAY'S *S. O. A. P.* STUDY

Scripture:

Matthew 5:10 Read, Write & Memorize

_____

_____

_____

_____

_____

_____

Observation:

What is God speaking to my heart as I read?

_____

_____

_____

_____

_____

_____

TODAY'S *S.O.A.P.* STUDY

Application:

How does this truth apply to my call to follow Jesus?

_____

_____

_____

_____

_____

_____

Prayer:

In light of what God has shown me, how do I need to pray?

_____

_____

_____

_____

_____

_____

DAY 20

Reward in Heaven

"Treasures can only be laid up in heaven when they have been laid down on earth."

G. Raymond Carlson

"Blessed are you when people insult you, persecute you and falsely say all kinds of evil against you because of me. Rejoice and be glad, because great is your reward in heaven, for in the same way they persecuted the prophets who were before you."—Matthew 5:11-12

God's people will be the richest people on the planet. Wealth in the Kingdom of God is not measured by worldly standards of success but by heavenly rewards. The apostle Paul describes the rewards as a crown of righteousness (2 Timothy 4:8). The persecuted will be rewarded by God either on earth or in Heaven or both (Revelation 21-22). The most important wealth to accumulate on earth will be received in heaven. These specific rewards are a future guarantee as a result of living a life marked by godly character in the present age. You will experience God's approval of your endurance through persecution when He rewards you with eternal life in His presence in the age to come. He will not forget those moments when you stood firm for His kingdom on earth. The blessing of God is found in moments of persecution, and the rewards of God will be followed by moments of joy. The future joy of receiving rewards from God for persecution is available today. Some of the most joyful times on earth will follow the most painful times, because your joy is not based on unstable circumstances or people who fail, but on a God that is neither unshaken nor able to fail.

Rewards for being persecuted will not save your soul from Hell, which is eternal separation from God. As someone once put it, "Salvation depends upon Christ's work for us, while rewards depend upon our works for Christ." God created us for good works that result in rewards. Good works are the result of godly character. He does not save us because of our good works nor because of our rewards. He saves us because of our faith in Jesus' work on the cross, and His death that made eternal life possible for all those who believe in it. His death then allows us to live a life marked by godly character on earth. Jesus' work on the cross is the motivation for our good works. A good work is only a good work if there is proper motivation behind it. God will test the quality of our good works. Stanley Horton said, "The quality, not the quantity of every person's work will be tested for rewards." Those good works that pass the test will have love attached to them.

When you are persecuted, Jesus commands you not to simply endure it, but to experience it with deep joy, knowing that you are identifying with Jesus and all the prophets who have been persecuted throughout history. Every follower of Christ is responsible for the good works which God has prepared for them. Some of those good works will result in rewards from being persecuted. Others will not pass the test because they were done without character. The reality is that persecution can come from the home, neighborhood, workplace, and community when you live like Jesus. No one can reward you like Jesus. A wise person once said, "God is grooming you for heaven, just as He is preparing heaven for you." All good works have the potential to be tested and approved by God, even if they result in persecution. Rejoice and be glad because God has the final word when we suffer persecution.

Today's *Character* Dare

God dares you to rejoice and be glad when persecuted. He promises to reward your good works, especially enduring persecution for identifying with His life. Today, prayerfully resolve to do the right thing, even if it results in persecution.

TODAY'S *S. O. A. P.* STUDY

Scripture:

Matthew 5:11-12 Read, Write & Memorize

_____

_____

_____

_____

_____

_____

Observation:

What is God speaking to my heart as I read?

_____

_____

_____

_____

_____

TODAY'S *S. O. A. P.* STUDY

Application:

How does this truth apply to my call to follow Jesus?

_____

_____

_____

_____

_____

Prayer:

In light of what God has shown me, how do I need to pray?

_____

_____

_____

_____

_____

_____

DAY 21

Salt & Light

"Change is not merely necessary to life. It is life."
Alvin Toffler

"You are the salt of the earth....You are the light of the world."
—Matthew 5:13-16

God's people should be the most change-producing people on the planet. You are the salt of the earth. You move people to change. You are not influenced by any value system other than the Kingdom of God. In the ancient days, the form of salt Jesus had in mind in this passage was the salt used for agricultural purposes. As a fertilizer, it made things grow better. It was used specifically to make better compost piles. Salt's agricultural purpose was to make things flourish because it accelerates growth. Like salt, Christ followers must be engaged in and with culture so that their presence makes things better, fuller, and more robust. If you accommodate culture, you will become like salt that loses its distinctiveness, making yourself ineffective. The character of a disciple produces growth and change in the culture. You are the salt of your home, workplace, neighborhood, and community. There are not many things in life more purposeful than living as a catalyst. A catalyst is an agent of change. It is not consumed by others, but transforms everything around it. Your mission is to be a transforming agent in your sphere of influence.

Salty disciples are catalysts of human flourishing. Followers of Christ distribute their influence by connecting to culture without compromising their distinctiveness from the culture. Their presence in a room full of people should be the most real thing there. They do not participate in darkness but present a positive influence. They are dynamic because they accelerate growth. Their presence in a room of people is contagious. They are distinct because their relationship with God sustains their presence in culture. Their presence in a room full of people makes people want to be near because their presence is pure.

God's people should be the most visible people on the planet. You are the light of the world. You are an example of human goodness. If people want to know what it means to be human, they are to look to you. As a follower of Christ, you are made in the image and likeness of God. You were created to reflect God's character to the world. Since God is reality, then you're the most real thing people see. Light is attractive to those who benefit from its ability to make things visible. You are the light of your home, workplace, neighborhood, and community. The character of a disciple attracts people to Christ in the culture. There are not many things more purposeful than living as an example of human goodness. You are the embodiment of human goodness. Your mission is to be the most attractive person in your sphere of influence, a person of godly character that reflects genuine goodness in all directions: God, self, others, and the world.

Shining disciples are examples of human goodness. Followers of Christ disseminate their influence by their self-evident presence. Their presence in a room full of people cannot be ignored any more than can a lighthouse. Real apprentices of Jesus are dynamic because of their self-revelatory character. Their presence cannot be denied because everything is better now that they are there. Real apprentices are distinct because of their self-evident goodness. Their presence in a room full of people testifies to a life of genuine good deeds that explain Jesus' message without words. They broadcast a message that is both positive and good. The reality is that everyone broadcasts a message from his or her own hill. A hill is your sphere of influence. Allow your light to shine in your sphere of influence so "that they may see your good deeds and praise your Father in heaven" (Matthew 5:16).

TODAY'S *Character* DARE

God dares you to be life-changing salt on the earth and highly visible light in the world. Your character as a disciple of Christ produces positive change in people and influences their value systems. Today, prayerfully resolve to always reflect godly character.

TODAY'S *S.O.A.P.* STUDY

Scripture:

Matthew 5:13-16 Read, Write & Memorize

_____

_____

_____

_____

_____

_____

Observation:

What is God speaking to my heart as I read?

_____

_____

_____

_____

_____

_____

TODAY'S *S. O. A. P.* STUDY

Application:

How does this truth apply to my call to follow Jesus?

_____

_____

_____

_____

_____

_____

Prayer:

In light of what God has shown me, how do I need to pray?

_____

_____

_____

_____

_____

_____

DAY 22
Worship

"God is most glorified in us when we are most satisfied in Him."
John Piper

Then the eleven disciples went to Galilee, to the mountain where Jesus had told them to go. When they saw him, they worshiped Him; but some doubted. —Matthew 28:16-17

There is no one or nothing in life that should be worshipped other than Jesus. Worship of God is central to the Christian faith. After Jesus had risen from the dead, His disciples' first response was to worship Him. They did not evangelize or disciple anybody. They worshipped Jesus as the risen Lord. Then Jesus commissioned them to "make disciples of all nations" (Matthew 28:19). Worship preceded discipleship because discipleship flows out of worship. The best worshippers are the best disciplers.

"The word *worship* is a combination of two words...suggesting that worship is reverence paid to the One who is worthy," Richard Champion once said. God is the only one who is worthy of our worship. Worship results from satisfaction in God. The more satisfied we are with God, the more satisfied we will be living for God. Worship of God grounds discipleship in God. Worship and discipleship are interrelated. One affects the other. If you get worship wrong, then you will get discipleship wrong. As Benjamin B. Warfield so aptly put it, the purpose of worship is to glorify God and to enjoy Him forever. The purpose of discipleship is to enhance the glory of God among men and women. It does not matter if you are singing songs of worship to God or acting as a living song for God; you are glorifying God—giving Him your best.

Worship is the lifestyle of a disciple. The apostle Paul urges all followers of Christ "to offer your bodies as living sacrifices, holy and pleasing to God—this is your spiritual act of worship" (Romans 12:1). Paul redefined worship as a lifestyle. For Paul, all of life is worship not only when we sing worship songs. From the beginning, when the first humans were created in God's image and likeness, our bodies were designed to worship God. They were made to be in tune with God and His plans for human life. Sin altered our ability to fully worship God. Through the power of Christ's death and resurrection, we can worship God with every fiber of our being.

Worship is holy love for God, the focus of discipleship. Discipleship is holy love for others, the fruit of worship. John Piper says something extremely profound about worship: "God is most glorified in us when we are most satisfied in Him." In the Apostle Paul's letter to the Philippians, Paul says that he desired to be with Christ more than anything else (Philippians 1:21-23). Paul was most satisfied by God. He had deep affection for Christ. He experienced intimacy with Christ that was far greater than anything this world had to offer. Paul was completely satisfied in Christ, and God was most glorified. What satisfies you? What gives you fulfillment? If it is not Christ, then your worship will not show that Christ is magnificent; it will not exalt Christ and demonstrate that He is great. Your view and practice of worship will affect your life as a disciple.

TODAY'S *Commissioning* DARE

God dares you to have a lifestyle of worship. He commissions you to glorify Him and enjoy Him forever. Today, prayerfully resolve to make worshipping God the focus of your life.

TODAY'S *S. O. A. P.* STUDY

Scripture:

Matthew 28:16-17 Read, Write & Memorize

_____

_____

_____

_____

_____

_____

Observation:

What is God speaking to my heart as I read?

_____

_____

_____

_____

_____

_____

_____

TODAY'S *S.O.A.P.* STUDY

Application:

How does this truth apply to my call to follow Jesus?

_____

_____

_____

_____

_____

_____

Prayer:

In light of what God has shown me, how do I need to pray?

_____

_____

_____

_____

_____

_____

DAY 23
Authority

"This is the lofty claim. Our Lord, Jesus Christ, has all authority in heaven and on earth, because our Lord Jesus is God."

John Piper

Then Jesus came to them and said, "All authority in heaven and on earth has been given to me."—Matthew 28:18

There is no one with more authority in heaven or on earth than Jesus. He has chief executive rights. All the CEOs, presidents, and government officials do not have more power than Jesus. After He was resurrected from the dead, Jesus proclaimed to His disciples a promise of universal power validating his plan to disciple all nations. Jesus' authority is not new, but as His ministry progressed from his own baptism to His climactic post-resurrection commissioning of His disciples, so did His authority on earth. The emphasis does not fall on Jesus' resurrection, on His exaltation to Heaven, or His future coming as the Son of Man to judge and rule the world, but on the universal authority delegated to Him.

In the poem, "All Authority," John Piper writes, "He has authority over Satan and all demons, over all angels—good and evil—over the natural universe, natural objects and laws and forces: stars, galaxies, planets, meteorites…authority over all weather systems…authority over all molecular and atomic reality…authority over all plants and animals great and small…authority over all the parts and functions of the human body…authority over all nations and governments…" Jesus has all-encompassing authority in heaven and on earth.

There is no one who wanted to highjack Jesus' authority more than the Devil. Right before Jesus launched into public ministry, Satan tempted Him three times. The most significant temptation was the final one. In the third temptation, the most significant of three, all His authority was at risk. The Devil offered Jesus all the kingdoms of the world, if

Jesus would bow down and worship him (Matthew 5:8-9). The Devil wanted Jesus to be his servant, not God's. He wanted Jesus to be his Messiah, not God's. The Devil wanted Jesus to do things his way. The Devil wanted Jesus to take the easy street, the road without suffering, in order to prevent Him from accomplishing God's work. Jesus was not overcome by the Devil, but overcame the Devil by standing firm on the truth of God's word. Instead of compromising His conviction to do God's work, the Devil's way, He stood His ground and was committed to do God's work, God's way, no matter the cost.

The authority Jesus received from God is now lent to the Christian community. Jesus empowers His followers with the greatest authority known to mankind. It is the authority to make disciples who are catalysts of change and examples of human goodness. There is nothing more significant in life than to receive training for living the life of discipleship. The most powerful moments in a follower of Christ's life will be in the context of discipleship. There is no easy way or shortcut to discipling people in becoming fully devoted followers of Christ; it is only accomplished through the long and slow process of discipleship. There is no other life-changing process on earth more powerful for the life of a believer than discipleship. All authority was given to all members of the Christian community to make disciples, not just the pastors, deacons, and elders of a church. The only way the Church is going to change the world for Christ is if all followers of Christ exercise their authority as disciple makers.

TODAY'S *Commissioning* DARE

God dares Christ followers to receive Jesus' authority as the means by which disciples are made. All disciples are given all authority to reproduce the life of Christ in others. Today, prayerfully resolve to stand firm on the authority of God on earth in order to do God's work, God's way.

TODAY'S *S. O. A. P.* STUDY

Scripture:

Matthew 28:18 Read, Write & Memorize

Observation:

What is God speaking to my heart as I read?

TODAY'S *S. O. A. P.* STUDY

Application:

How does this truth apply to my call to follow Jesus?

_____

_____

_____

_____

_____

Prayer:

In light of what God has shown me, how do I need to pray?

_____

_____

_____

_____

_____

DAY 24

Making Disciples

"When I invited Jesus into my life, I thought he was going to put up some wallpaper and hang a few pictures. But he started knocking out walls and adding rooms. I said I was expecting a nice cottage but he said I'm making a palace in which to live."

C.S. Lewis

"Therefore go and make disciples of all nations, baptizing them in the name of the Father and of the Son and of the Holy Spirit..."—Matthew 28:19

There is no one in life more mission-minded than followers of Christ. The C.I.A., during the Cold War, had a code of conduct their agents followed called the Moscow Rules. One agent reported, "Although no one had written them down, they were the precepts we all understood... By the time they arrived in Moscow, everyone knew these rules. They were dead simple and full of common sense" (See en.wikipedia.org/wiki/The_Moscow_Rules). One of them was "know your mission." In the same way the Church needs to know its mission. The Church does not have a mission. The mission of God has a Church. The Church is the highway in which the mission of God travels on. To make more and better disciples is the method by which the Church fulfills the mission of God.

A disciple of Christ is simply a pupil, a learner, or an apprentice; one who follows someone else's teachings. To be a disciple means, above all, to follow after the lifestyle defined in the teachings of Jesus. A disciple of Christ reproduces his or her Christlikeness in others. A disciple is part of a community because discipleship is a community issue. Every time people were discipled in the New Testament, they were connected to a community of believers. Jesus organized His followers in groups of two, eleven, twelve, fifty, seventy, seventy-two and one hundred twenty. No one was ever discipled by himself. According to Greg Ogden, the central method by which the Church fulfills the mission of God is by leading people to become self-reproducing, fully devoted followers of Christ. The result of the mission of God is disciples of Christ who are fully reflective image bearers. If you get the mission wrong, you will not accomplish the central goal of the Church. You will experience mission drift; you will end up where you don't want to go, doing what you don't want to be doing. Therefore, you must not only know your mission, but be laser-focused on it.

One of the last things Jesus told His followers before He ascended into Heaven was His mission for the Church, "go and make disciples." What if you were a parent who told your children to take out the garbage before you return from running errands? You leave to run errands mostly for your children. When you return home you find the garbage has not been taken out. How would you feel? How do you think Jesus will feel when He returns for His church and the one thing He asked us to do we have not done to the best of our ability? There is no excuse acceptable for us not to make disciples. If you call yourself a follower of Christ, then your mission is to make disciples.

In the book, *The Path*, Laurie Beth Jones tells a war story. Those who got away from their platoon and got caught stumbling around were asked, "What is your mission?" And if they did not know it, they were killed. What if followers of Christ do not know the mission? Be careful of getting caught not completing your mission!

TODAY'S *Commissioning* DARE

God dares you to make discipleship a priority. Jesus has been given all authority for His followers to make disciples of all nations. Today, prayerfully resolve to stay laser-focused on making disciples.

TODAY'S *S. O. A. P.* STUDY

Scripture:

Matthew 28:19 Read, Write & Memorize

_____

_____

_____

_____

_____

_____

Observation:

What is God speaking to my heart as I read?

_____

_____

_____

_____

_____

_____

TODAY'S *S. O. A. P.* STUDY

Application:

How does this truth apply to my call to follow Jesus?

_____

_____

_____

_____

_____

_____

Prayer:

In light of what God has shown me, how do I need to pray?

_____

_____

_____

_____

_____

_____

_____

Water Baptism

"In baptism we are initiated, crowned, chosen, embraced, washed, adopted, gifted, reborn, killed, and thereby sent forth and redeemed. We are identified as one of God's own, then assigned our place and our job within the Kingdom of God."

William Willimon

"Therefore go and make disciples of all nations, baptizing them in the name of the Father and of the Son and of the Holy Spirit..."—Matthew 28:19

There is nothing in life more radical than taking the first step into discipleship. New recruits in the Marines pledge their allegiance to the military when they enlist. Immediately they begin to live radically different lives. The difference starts in the initiation process. The radical first step into the military through the rigors of boot camp shapes the rest of the recruits' time in the Marines. If the first step were not life-changing, then each step that followed would not be either. In the same way, a community called to "make disciples" initiates baptism as a radical first step in a lifelong process of teaching obedience to Jesus' commands.

In the first century, when new converts pledged allegiance to God the Father, the Son, and the Holy Spirit through the act of baptism, their lives were on the line. All those who took the early step into the Christian faith through public baptism knew they might suffer death as Jesus did. Many died because they forsook the culturally acceptable gods and religions of the Roman Empire. The very pledge Jesus made to God which led to His death is the same pledge Jesus expects His followers to make—the pledge of total allegiance to God.

Participating in the act of baptism is a public profession of your decision to follow Christ. In baptism, you identify with Christ's death and resurrection. The apostle Paul describes baptism "...having been buried with him in baptism and raised with him through your faith in the power of God, who raised him from the dead" (Colossians 2:12). When you are baptized by immersion, the act of completely going down into the water symbolizes your old self dying. Rising out of the water symbolizes your new life in Christ. The Apostle Paul describes it like this, "Therefore, if anyone is in Christ, he is a new creation; the old has gone, the new has come" (2 Corinthians 5:17). Baptism is a life-transforming experience. The old is in the past, and the new is in the future. This is a model for daily living.

The Great Commission is a call to make disciples who begin early on in their apprenticeship with baptism and then spend their entire lives learning and obeying the teachings of Christ. One of the very first acts of obedience commanded by Jesus is baptism. Jesus was baptized, He commanded His followers to be baptized and it was the practice of the early church throughout the book of Acts. There are few acts a new convert can participate in that solidify his or her decision to follow Christ as baptism does. If disciple-making communities neglect to properly lead converts into the disciple-making process through baptism, then these misled converts will not teach new disciples the importance of baptism. It is the responsibility of every follower of Christ to be baptized and then to lead others to baptism. Are you leading people in your faith community to baptism?

TODAY'S *Commissioning* DARE

God dares you to live radically. The first step is baptism, a radical initiation into the Christian faith. Today, prayerfully resolve to be water baptized or, if you have already done so, to encourage others to do the same.

TODAY'S *S. O. A. P.* STUDY

Scripture:

Matthew 28:19 Read, Write & Memorize

_____

_____

_____

_____

_____

_____

Observation:

What is God speaking to my heart as I read?

_____

_____

_____

_____

_____

_____

TODAY'S *S.O.A.P.* STUDY

Application:

How does this truth apply to my call to follow Jesus?

_____

_____

_____

_____

_____

_____

Prayer:

In light of what God has shown me, how do I need to pray?

_____

_____

_____

_____

_____

_____

DAY 26

Community Baptism

"The doctrine of the Trinity overloads our mental circuits. Despite its cognitive difficulty, however, this astonishing, dynamic conception of the triune God is bristling with profound, wonderful, life-shaping, world-changing implications."

Timothy Keller

"Therefore go and make disciples of all nations, baptizing them in the name of the Father and of the Son and of the Holy Spirit..."—Matthew 28:19

There is nothing more life-giving than relationship in God's community. Jesus' call for His disciples to baptize converts into the name of the Father, the Son, and the Holy Spirit is more than just a formula to repeat when immersing new believers in water. It is a pledge to live in relationship with God. Some two thousand years ago, when the early Church was birthed, it was extremely dangerous for followers of Christ to identify with the God of the Christians. Pledging allegiance to this God was risky. It was outside the norm. In those days, most people believed in many gods. In the beginning, the God of Christianity was permitted because it was just considered another god. Persecution began when the Romans discovered that Christians would not profess faith in the Roman state religion. The Christians rejected the so-called "gods" of the Roman Empire, because to them Jesus was the unique Son of God, "the way and the truth and the life" (John 14:6). Jesus' statement does exclude anybody who refuses to confess Him as Lord. The early Christians would later be persecuted for their allegiance to a God who is three persons yet one being. But as the early Christians would find out, their dangerous love affair with God was not suicidal, but life-giving.

God is a community of life-giving love. The inner life of God is a community of three persons: the Father, the Son and the Holy Spirit. Each person in the Trinity does not relate to the others by self-centered,

106

selfish love but by mutually self-giving, selfless love. Followers of Christ are not only baptized in water, but into a relationship with a God that is marked by self-giving love. The inner life of God grounds our life in community with others. The result of baptism into the community of God is radical life transformation of the way we relate to others in community. Since sacrificial love is at the core of the love that the Father, the Son, and the Holy Spirit have for one another, it is to be at the heart of the Christian community. Sacrificial love is a radical love, a dangerous and risky love for one another. It demands us not to be the center of attention, but to center our lives on the lives of others. In sacrificial love, your world revolves around others. Jesus is our model of someone who orbited around others.

Jesus gave His life for humanity in obedience to the eternal plan ordained by God the Father, Son and Holy Spirit. Yet for a moment, just before He gave Himself over to death on the cross, God incarnate showed the world how human He really was. In the Garden of Gethsemane, He cried out to His disciples, "…'My soul is overwhelmed with sorrow to the point of death. Stay here and keep watch with me.' Going a little farther, he fell with his face to the ground and prayed, 'My Father, if it is possible, may this cup be taken from me. Yet not as I will, but as you will'" (Matthew 26:38-39). Jesus felt the weight of the cross. In one breath, He's not afraid, but in another, He showed how committed He was to loving His Father. He was committed to the point of sacrifice. Sacrifice is only a sacrifice if it costs you something. For Jesus, it inevitably cost His life. What has it cost you lately?

TODAY'S *Commissioning* DARE

God dares you to live sacrificially. The Trinitarian love that the Son has for the Father and Holy Spirit shows us what it looks like to love those close to us. Today, prayerfully resolve to love people sacrificially no matter what it costs you.

TODAY'S *S. O. A. P.* STUDY

Scripture:

Matthew 28:19 Read, Write & Memorize

_____

_____

_____

_____

_____

_____

Observation:

What is God speaking to my heart as I read?

_____

_____

_____

_____

_____

_____

TODAY'S *S. O. A. P.* STUDY

<u>A</u>pplication:

How does this truth apply to my call to follow Jesus?

_____

_____

_____

_____

_____

_____

<u>P</u>rayer:

In light of what God has shown me, how do I need to pray?

_____

_____

_____

_____

_____

_____

DAY 27

Teaching

"To teach is to create a space in which obedience to truth is practiced."

Father Felix

"And teaching them to obey everything I have commanded you. And surely I am with you always, to the very end of the age."—Matthew 28:20

There is nothing in life more rigorous than training to be a follower of Christ. Marines are reprogrammed for war. They rigorously train in order to respond like a combatant, not a civilian. Jesus' training program for His followers is grounded in His teachings. Jesus' teaching reprograms His followers to respond to life as He would. Everything Jesus taught shaped and formed untrained, undisciplined people into fully devoted disciples. Jesus' teachings are the fulfillment of the entire Old Testament. He boldly said, "Do not think that I have come to abolish the Law or the Prophets; I have not come to abolish them but to fulfill them" (Matthew 5:17). Jesus' teachings are the climax and the goal of the Old Testament law. Jesus validates the law, but also fulfills it. His authority is unlike that of Moses, Jewish rabbis or anyone else. Only God has given Jesus executive rights over every square inch of the world. There is no one with more authority than Jesus to administer the teachings of God. Followers of Christ are to be committed to death to the teachings of Jesus, never to compromise for another training program. What would happen if Marines compromised their loyalty to their training? They would not only risk their own lives, but compromise the mission altogether.

The best Marines stick to the plan. They do not oppose authority, but choose to obey. They do not delay obedience, but through immediate obedience are made into the most elite military branch. Delayed obedience to Jesus' teaching is disobedience. The mission of God on earth will be compromised if His followers do not follow orders. Jesus modeled obedience in the face of death while on the cross. He obeyed His own teachings, such as love your enemy, in the heat of battle. He did not shrink back when the going got tough. He did not only obey when it was convenient, but also in the most inconvenient moments. The depth of your training will only show in the heat of battle, when your neighbor has a problem with you, when you are tempted to sin, or when you are fed up with a family member. The battle will either show your readiness or your laziness. Those who are the most ready for battle become the best at training others.

Every follower of Christ is responsible for training the next generation. Since everything you do or say can teach others, your life will either model immediate obedience, delayed obedience or disobedience to the teachings of Christ. William Graves, the editor of National Geographic magazine, said, "Years ago, after a celebrated international career on the stage, the world-famous violinist Jascha Heifetz became a professor of music at UCLA. When someone asked him why he had left the glamour of performing to become a teacher, Heifetz answered, 'Violin-playing is a perishable art. It must be passed on; otherwise it is lost.' Then he went on to say, 'I remember my old violin professor in Russia. He said that if I worked hard enough someday I would be good enough to teach.'" The hard work in training leads to the hard work on stage, qualifying you for the hard work of teaching. Every follower of Christ teaches the future generations obedience through the obedience to faith. Without teachers of the faith we are only one generation from extinction. Whom have you taught lately?.

TODAY'S *Commissioning* DARE

God dares you to teach radical obedience. The more radically obedient you are to God, the more radical your example will teach others to be. Today, prayerfully resolve to rigorously train for life's battles by radically obeying Jesus' teachings with no delay.

TODAY'S *S.O.A.P.* STUDY

Scripture:

Matthew 28:20 Read, Write & Memorize

_____

_____

_____

_____

_____

_____

Observation:

What is God speaking to my heart as I read?

_____

_____

_____

_____

_____

_____

TODAY'S *S.O.A.P.* STUDY

Application:

How does this truth apply to my call to follow Jesus?

_____

_____

_____

_____

_____

_____

Prayer:

In light of what God has shown me, how do I need to pray?

_____

_____

_____

_____

_____

_____

DAY 28

Presence of God

God's "center is everywhere, His circumference is nowhere."

Empedocles

"And teaching them to obey everything I have commanded you. And surely I am with you always, to the very end of the age."—Matthew 28:20

There is no one in life more committed to the mission of the church than the Holy Spirit. The mission of the church is not a solo act. Jesus promises His authority, His community, and His presence wherever you go to make disciples. Whether you are in your home, workplace, neighborhood, or community, He is with you. Jesus promises to be part of the process through His abiding presence. This idea is rooted in the Old Testament. According to Terence L. Donaldson, often in the Old Testament, the Lord promised to be with individuals or the people as a whole in order to pledge His assistance, comfort, and strength. The Lord told Moses, "I will be with you. And this will be the sign to you that it is I who have sent you: When you have brought the people out of Egypt, you will worship God on this mountain" (Exodus 3:11-12). Up until that point, Moses was not buying into God's plans. God wanted Moses to rescue the Israelites who were enslaved by Egypt. He was not confident in himself until the Lord promised His presence would be with him.

Moses was an ordinary person. He did not have a fancy resume. He actually had a criminal record for killing an Egyptian a few years before his calling (Exodus 2:1-20). For the first forty years of his life, Moses was in the land of Egypt. For the next forty years Moses was in the desert. And for the final forty years Moses was in the service of God. He learned that for the first forty years, he was a somebody, for the next forty years, he was a nobody, and for the final forty years of his life, he learned how God could take a nobody and make him into a somebody. Because of the presence of God, ordinary Moses did extraordinary things. Moses had next to nothing when he started God's mission. According to Exodus 4:2, "The LORD said to him, 'What is that in your hand?' 'A staff,' he replied." Moses had so little with him that he was forced to rely on the presence of God. God used Moses with only a staff to save a nation from oppression. If Moses did not obey God, the nation of Israel might not have been delivered in that generation. God would have found someone else to do the job, but why should it not be Moses? Even if the only thing you have in your hand is a staff like Moses, you can still bring change to the world.

The mission of God is impossible without God. God's presence makes the mission possible. Without God working through the disciple-making process, an untrained, undisciplined person will have neither hope nor chance of becoming a fully devoted follower of Christ. The maturity of a believer is exclusively the work of God, not anyone else. The Apostle Paul made this clear by saying, "So neither he who plants nor he who waters is anything, but only God, who makes things grow" (1 Corinthians 3:7). People plant the seeds and water them, but God causes the increase. He makes the seed grow and mature into a beautiful plant. He is the only one who could lead an unrepentant person to repentance. The disciple-making process does not ultimately rest on His followers but on God, causing the person to grow to maturity in Christ. God's people play a significant part, but their efforts are limited. The power of God completes the work of making disciples through God's partnership with His people. Jesus designed His ministry plans on His promise of power, community, and presence. The disciple-making process will not conclude until Jesus returns for His church. Are you part of the disciple-making process?

TODAY'S *Commissioning* DARE

God dares you to rely on His presence to make disciples. Converts aren't made into disciples without God's power. Today, prayerfully resolve to depend on the power of God in the process of making disciples of all nations, no matter how impossible the task seems.

TODAY'S *S. O. A. P.* STUDY

Scripture:

Matthew 28:20 Read, Write & Memorize

_____

_____

_____

_____

_____

_____

Observation:

What is God speaking to my heart as I read?

_____

_____

_____

_____

_____

_____

TODAY'S *S. O. A. P.* STUDY

Application:

How does this truth apply to my call to follow Jesus?

_____

_____

_____

_____

_____

_____

Prayer:

In light of what God has shown me, how do I need to pray?

_____

_____

_____

_____

_____

_____

SECTION 4

THE COMMUNITY LIFE
OF A DISCIPLE

DAY 29

Gone Fishing

"Give a man a fish, he'll eat for a day. Teach a man how to fish, he'll eat for a lifetime."

Ancient Proverb

As Jesus was walking beside the Sea of Galilee, he saw two brothers, Simon called Peter and his brother Andrew. They were casting a net into the lake, for they were fishermen. "Come, follow me," Jesus said, "and I will make you fishers of men."—Matthew 4:18-19

Jesus called you to be His disciple in order for you to call others to discipleship. He compared the process to fishing. In the first century, commercial fishermen used nets to catch fish. Fishing for the first disciples was neither a hobby nor a sport, but a way of life. It was not something scheduled in calendars when there was nothing left to do. It was the main activity. All of life revolved around fishing. If they did not fish, they would not have a product to sell. If they did not profit, they would go without. Jesus knew that if these first disciples were going to understand what it took to follow Him, He had to use something in their life powerful enough to catch their attention. Most people today do not work for a fishing business, but the metaphor still speaks volumes to the discipleship process.

If we are going to follow in Jesus' footsteps as the "Great Fisherman," we must understand that discipleship is neither a hobby, nor a ministry, nor a program. Like a career fisherman, it is a lifestyle. Following Jesus in our everyday lives is the most important thing to do each day. Few things are more important in life than regularly leading people into fully devoted followers of Christ.

There is great skill involved in fishing. Today, it's customary for sports fishermen to fish with bait instead of nets. Having the right bait increases the likelihood of a good catch. Jesus left us with two pieces of bait. If we do not have the right bait we will leave the pond empty-handed. The bait every Christ follower must utilize is speaking the right words and doing the right works. Every fisherman's best friend is the Holy Spirit who prepares the ears of the people and makes it attractive to them. Saying the right things and doing the right things will help you catch boatloads of fish. However, if your words and works are not delivered in the right way, they might run the fish off, and you might not ever be able to go back to your fishing hole.

Most of the time you will only have one opportunity to make a first impression. If your bait intersects with a fish and it does not smell right or the circumstance does not look right, then the fish will leave. Every time you throw your bait you are calling people into discipleship. Every word you speak or work you do evangelizes. Either you will give them a reason to follow, or you will give them a reason not to respond to Jesus' call to discipleship. Everything teaches. Everything disciples. Everywhere you go, there is an invisible sign on you, that says, "Gone fishing."

TODAY'S *Community Life* DARE

God dares you to go on a permanent fishing trip! Every word or work done by a Christ follower will either lead people to Jesus or deter people from Jesus. Today, prayerfully resolve to live your life as a fulltime fisher of men and women, not seasonal or part-time helpers.

TODAY'S *S. O. A. P.* STUDY

Scripture:

Matthew 4:18-19 Read, Write & Memorize

_____

_____

_____

_____

_____

_____

Observation:

What is God speaking to my heart as I read?

_____

_____

_____

_____

_____

_____

TODAY'S *S. O. A. P.* STUDY

Application:

How does this truth apply to my call to follow Jesus?

_____

_____

_____

_____

_____

_____

Prayer:

In light of what God has shown me, how do I need to pray?

_____

_____

_____

_____

_____

_____

DAY 30

Words of the Heart

"As human beings, we use words to communicate, and the words we use describe and depict the pictures that we hold in our heart."

Rebekah Harkness

For out of the overflow of the heart the mouth speaks. —*Matthew 12:34*

God's people should use the most meaningful words on the planet. Words are very telling. They show what you are like on the inside. People tend to talk about the things that most interest them. Most people cannot help themselves but to share what most excites them. People also cannot help but respond to life circumstances verbally. When someone hits their funny bone, they usually show you through a verbal knee-jerk response what they are like on the inside. The mouth is the voice piece of the heart. Words communicate the condition of our hearts either consciously or subconsciously. Words from our hearts find themselves into the minds of others, so choose carefully.

God designed the disciple-making process to be communicated verbally. Followers of Christ train others by speaking words of instruction. They coach others by speaking words of encouragement. They pastor others by speaking words of correction. Every word counts. By using words loosely, they can turn others away from the faith. They can reinforce destructive speaking habits in the culture instead of challenging them with Jesus' style of speaking. But most importantly they can cause you to sin. The apostle James says, "With the tongue we praise our Lord and Father, and with it we curse men, who have been made in God's likeness. Out of the same mouth comes praise and cursing. My brothers, this should not be. Can both fresh water and salt water flow from the same spring? My brothers, can a fig tree bear olives, or a grapevine bear figs? Neither can a salt spring produce fresh water (James 3:9-12)." The person who praises God should not use words loosely, but choose words wisely.

Jesus' death saved not only your soul, but also your tongue. The apostle Peter spoke words out of the abundance of his heart that he regretted. At a fire, after Jesus was arrested, Peter, with wavering faith, failed to stand up for Christ when asked three times about his association. On the third occasion, Peter not only denied following Jesus, but cursed as well (Matthew 26:69-75). His heart convicted him as he wept bitterly. But after the Holy Spirit came to him on the day of Pentecost, Peter was one out of the 120 who stood up and spoke boldly out of the overflow of his heart. The Bible tells us "3,000 were added to their number that day" (Acts 2:41). What if Peter's heart had not been changed, and he hadn't trained his tongue to proclaim Jesus as Lord and Savior? He would have missed a great opportunity to witness the power of God. Instead of showing a heart hardened to God like he did at the fire, he showed a heart on fire for God. What opportunities have you missed when you have gone fishing because your heart was not in the right place and the wrong words spewed out of it?

TODAY'S *Community Life* DARE

God dares you to control your tongue. Controlling your tongue is a heart issue. If you allow garbage in, garbage will come out. Practice self-control today by keeping your heart in the right place with God and therefore avoiding hurtful words. Today, prayerfully resolve only to speak words that communicate value to God and His people.

TODAY'S *S.O.A.P.* STUDY

Scripture:

Matthew 12:34 Read, Write & Memorize

_____

_____

_____

_____

_____

_____

Observation:

What is God speaking to my heart as I read?

_____

_____

_____

_____

_____

_____

TODAY'S *S. O. A. P.* STUDY

Application:

How does this truth apply to my call to follow Jesus?

_____

_____

_____

_____

_____

_____

_____

Prayer:

In light of what God has shown me, how do I need to pray?

_____

_____

_____

_____

_____

_____

_____

DAY 31
Truthful Words

"You can fool some of the people all of the time, and all of the people some of the time, but you cannot fool all of the people all of the time."

Abraham Lincoln

"Again, you have heard that it was said to the people long ago, 'Do not break your oath, but keep the oaths you have made to the Lord.' But I tell you, 'Do not swear at all: either by heaven, for it is God's throne; or by the earth, for it is his footstool; or by Jerusalem, for it is the city of the Great King. And do not swear by your head, for you cannot make even one hair white or black. Simply let your 'Yes' be 'Yes,' and your 'No,' 'No;' anything beyond this comes from the evil one."—Matthew 5:33-37

God's people should be the most honest people on the planet. Honesty is not just the best policy but the only policy in God's Kingdom. In this passage, Jesus dispelled the traditional practice of swearing on things that exclusively belong to God. They swore on heaven, earth, Jerusalem, and even their own heads. Jesus' contemporaries swore upon such things in order to validate their word. They lacked verbal integrity because others knew they would often lie. Jesus overruled these practices, teaching us to be reliable in our words without the support of an oath. Jesus made it clear that nothing validates one's words but the condition of the heart. As David Turner said, "If one's heart is right with God, upright speech will transparently represent what is in one's heart."

Telling the truth is a testament to the character of a disciple, but lying destroys credibility with outsiders. Disciples who tell the truth identify with the father of truth, Jesus, but those who lie identify with the father of lies, Satan (John 8:44). Truth is part of a disciple's DNA. A disciple who does not tell the truth will live a life of deception. Ultimately, he or she only deceives him or herself. But a disciple who lives truthfully with all people will live a life of freedom. There is no freedom outside of facing the truth in any situation. Jesus clearly connected truth-telling and freedom when He said," you will know the truth, and the truth will set you free" (Matthew 8:32). The people who are the most honest are the most used in the Kingdom of God. While you "fish" in your home, workplace, neighborhood, or community, share the truth all of the time. Honesty builds a bridge of truth to the hearts of people. If they can trust you, then they can trust your message.

Living untruthfully not only weakens your witness, but hinders your spiritual growth. Disciples of Christ will only grow spiritually to the degree they speak honestly with themselves, God, and others. There is a story of a follower of Christ who decided not to share the last ten percent—hurts, hang-ups, and habits. He told most people, most of the truth, most of the time, but held back the last ten percent. At times, he mustered up the strength and courage to share ninety percent of his life, but only sharing ninety percent of the truth stunted his growth, preventing him from ever prevailing over his addiction to alcohol. Two decades of only sharing the ninety percent left him in a pickle. Not sharing the final ten percent destroyed his family, his trust with people he respected dearly, and most importantly his trust with God. When confronted about the secret part of his life, he tried to hide behind the same lies, but then suddenly he broke the cycle by telling the truth. He became completely transparent to the people that mattered most, escaping the bondage of a life-controlling addiction. Honesty opens the door to life change. Who knows the last ten percent in your life?

TODAY'S *Community Life* DARE

God dares you to speak truthfully to all people all the time. Your words mean nothing if your heart is full of deceit. Never swear on anything, but always speak openly and honestly with everyone. Today, prayerfully resolve to tell the truth at all times, no matter what.

TODAY'S *S. O. A. P.* STUDY

Scripture:

Matthew 5:33-37 Read, Write & Memorize

_____

_____

_____

_____

_____

_____

Observation:

What is God speaking to my heart as I read?

_____

_____

_____

_____

_____

_____

TODAY'S *S.O.A.P.* STUDY

Application:

How does this truth apply to my call to follow Jesus?

_____

_____

_____

_____

_____

_____

Prayer:

In light of what God has shown me, how do I need to pray?

_____

_____

_____

_____

_____

_____

DAY 32

Vain Words

"The name of God is Holy because it is self given."
Matthew J. Slick

You shall not misuse the name of the LORD your God, for the LORD will not hold anyone guiltless who misuses his name. —*Exodus 20:7*

God's people should honor the name of God more than anyone on the planet. If God's people do not respect the name of God, then the non-believer surely will not. The unbeliever learns how to honor the name of God by the way believers honor God's name. Today the third commandment (stated above) may be the most ignored because we often hear people using the name of God in vain. According to Matthew J. Slick, to misuse God's name means literally "to lift it up to or attach it to emptiness." The name of God is not to be used in this manner. God did not obtain His name from some group of people; He revealed His own name. Therefore, the name of God is sacred. The name was so sacred that God's people did not speak it when reading the Scripture. They used an alternative Hebrew name for God, *Adonai*, which means Lord or master. The name of God was the most holy word in their vocabulary. No one took it for granted, going to extreme measures to protect its holiness.

God's name has always existed. He knows who He is. He is the Eternal One, the Creator, the one who has always been and who will always be. He is the great "*I AM*." Out of God's own nature, out of His own heart, He disclosed His holy name to us. It is self-given. His name is holy and is not to be used in a irreverent way. Thus, as Matthew J. Slick states, God commands us not to use His name in vain. Jesus reaffirmed the third commandment in the prayer He taught His disciples. He began it by saying, "Our Father in heaven, hallowed be your name…" (Matthew 6:9). As David Turner says, God's name represents His person and His character. His will on earth flows out of His character. Honoring God's name requires not only reverence for it, but also participation in the advancement of His kingdom and proclaiming who He is to those who have not heard. God's mission on earth requires His followers to honor His name while serving in His kingdom.

The mission of God on earth is for His name to be hallowed (or honored) by people's allegiance and obedience to Him. The more God's name is honored on earth, the further God's Kingdom will reach. If God's name is only popular in our jokes or curses, then God's kingdom suffers. The ultimate fulfillment of God's name will be in the Second Coming of Christ when God's Kingdom is fully realized on earth.

Even General Robert E. Lee did not allow his name to be used in vain. After the American Civil War the managers of the infamous Louisiana Lottery approached General Lee and asked if he would let them use his name in their scheme. They promised that if he did, he would become rich. Astounded, Lee straightened up, buttoned his gray coat, and shouted, "Gentlemen, I lost my home in the war. I lost my fortune in the war. I lost everything except my name. My name is not for sale…" God's name is not for sale, only for honoring, anything else is off-limits for the name of God.

TODAY'S *Community Life* DARE

God dares you not to use His name in vain. Be careful to treat His name with reverence and respect and others will follow. Today, prayerfully resolve to live a lifestyle that honors the Lord's name, not attaching emptiness but reverence to it.

TODAY'S *S. O. A. P.* STUDY

Scripture:

Exodus 20:7 Read, Write & Memorize

_____

_____

_____

_____

_____

_____

Observation:

What is God speaking to my heart as I read?

_____

_____

_____

_____

_____

_____

TODAY'S *S. O. A. P.* STUDY

Application:

How does this truth apply to my call to follow Jesus?

_____

_____

_____

_____

_____

Prayer:

In light of what God has shown me, how do I need to pray?

_____

_____

_____

_____

_____

DAY 33
Edifying Words

"Gossip and slander are not victimless crimes. Words do not just dissipate into midair...Words can injure and damage, maim and destroy - forcefully, painfully, lastingly...Plans have been disrupted, deals have been lost, companies have fallen, because of idle gossip or malicious slander. Reputations have been sullied, careers have been ruined, lives have been devastated, because of cruel lies or vicious rumors...Your words have such power to do good or evil that they must be chosen carefully, wisely, and well."

Wayne Dosick

Do not let any unwholesome talk come out of your mouths, but only what is helpful for building others up according to their needs, that it may benefit those who listen. —Ephesians 4:29

God's people should be the most edifying people on the planet. The word *edify* means to build up. The word *unwholesome* means rotten or spoiled. Words either build people up or tear them down and spoil them. Words set the tone, sending a positive or negative message. Words help people meet needs or hinder needs from being met. As Gary Chapman has said, "Verbal compliments, or words of appreciation, are powerful communicators of love." Unwholesome words are powerful communicators of apathy—the opposite of love.

Edifying words indirectly proclaim God's love. Using words that build up in conversations at work or in your neighbor's house reveals your character. People are attracted to those who build them up. But those who tear others down may not have a voice in other people's lives and may lose their chance to express God's love. Who can hear a message of love, when every other word destroys? Absolutely no one! Verbal communication that edifies helps you earn the right to speak into your neighbor's or co-worker's life. Sprinkling your conversations with encouraging, humble, and kind words instead of negative gossip or curse words, says something about your heart. People do not necessarily trust your words as much as they trust your heart. People trust the message, if they trust the messenger. The heart that seeks to love others with edifying words will be able to effectively communicate God's message.

Unwholesome words destroy relationships. Never put your "Gone Fishing" sign up if your conversation is sprinkled with rotten and spoiled words. A study was conducted on newlyweds over their first decade of marriage. The researchers found a very subtle but telling difference at the beginning of the relationships. Among couples who would ultimately stay together, five out of every one hundred comments made about each other were putdowns. Among couples that would later split, ten of every one hundred comments were insults. That gap magnified over the following decade, until couples heading downhill were flinging five times as many cruel and invalidating comments at each other as happy couples. "Hostile putdowns act as cancerous cells that, if unchecked, erode the relationship over time," says Dr. Clifford Notarius in *U.S. News and World Report*. Conversation that is cancerous will kill any opportunities for sharing Christ, but conversation that is edifying will always point people to Christ. Are your conversations sprinkled with cancerous or edifying words?

TODAY'S *Community Life* DARE

God dares you to always build people up. Only speak edifying words. Never choose words inconsistent with God's heart. Today, prayerfully resolve never to speak a foul word but only words that are kind, encouraging, and compassionate.

TODAY'S *S. O. A. P.* STUDY

Scripture:

Ephesians 4:29 Read, Write & Memorize

_____

_____

_____

_____

_____

_____

Observation:

What is God speaking to my heart as I read?

_____

_____

_____

_____

_____

_____

TODAY'S *S. O. A. P.* STUDY

Application:

How does this truth apply to my call to follow Jesus?

_____

_____

_____

_____

_____

_____

Prayer:

In light of what God has shown me, how do I need to pray?

_____

_____

_____

_____

_____

_____

DAY 34

Gentle Words

*"Love is kind. If then we are to communicate love
verbally, we must use kind words."*

Gary Chapman

A gentle answer turns away wrath, but a harsh word stirs up anger.
—*Proverbs 15:1*

God's people should be the most gentle people on the planet. Tone matters. Gentle words set the stage for others to listen while harsh words shut down the conversation. Non-verbal communication matters. Peter Drucker put it this way: "The most important thing in communication is hearing what isn't being said." Communicating is not only about what we say but about the way we say it. People in the office or grocery store hear the non-verbal communication over your words. There are three components of communication: (1) Verbal (what we say) - seven percent of any message is communicated through words, (2) Vocal (how we say it) - thirty-eight percent of a message is communicated by our voice, and (3) Visual (what our body says) - fifty-five percent is conveyed by non-verbal body language (UCLA Study). Non-verbal communication makes up ninety-three percent of a conversation. Gentleness matters.

There was a story about children who won four free goldfish at a school carnival. Early Saturday morning, the family was off to the local pet store in search of an aquarium. They chose a used ten-gallon tank for a bargain of five dollars. The father said, "Of course, it was nasty, but the savings made the two hours of cleanup a breeze. Those four new fish looked great in their new home, at least for the first day. But by Sunday one had died. Too bad, but three remained. Monday morning revealed a second casualty, and by Monday night a third goldfish had gone belly up." They asked a friend who had a 30 gallon tank to assess their situation. It didn't take him long to discover the problem. The father soon realized, "I had washed the tank with soap, an absolute no-no. My uninformed efforts had destroyed the very lives I was trying to protect." In our efforts to clean up our own lives or the lives of others, we use "killer soaps"—harsh words, condemnation, criticism, nagging, and fits of temper. As Robert J. Morgan says, we think we're doing right, but our harsh tone and self-righteous treatment is more than people can bear.

According to Morgan, there are five keys to gentleness when in conversation. First, actively seek to make others feel at ease. Be sensitive and welcoming to others' opinions and ideas. Secondly, show respect for the personal dignity of the other person. When you need to change a wrong opinion, do so with persuasion and kindness rather than domination or intimidation. Thirdly, avoid blunt speech and abrupt manner. Be sensitive to how others react to your words, considering how they may feel. Fourthly, don't be threatened by opposition; gently instruct, asking God to dissolve the opposition. Fifthly, do not belittle or degrade a brother (or sister) who has fallen by gossiping—instead grieve and pray for his (or her) repentance. The gentlest people might not say a lot, but are extremely in tune to the needs of others. The gentle person earns the right to speak into the lives of his or her neighbors, co-workers, and others in the community. Always "go fishing" for people with a gentle word.

TODAY'S *Community Life* DARE

God dares you to always communicate gentleness. Only the gentle person wins the argument. Use no harsh words but words that communicate loving kindness. Today, prayerfully resolve to always be mindful of others when communicating.

TODAY'S *S.O.A.P.* STUDY

Scripture:

Proverbs 15:1 Read, Write & Memorize

_____

_____

_____

_____

_____

_____

Observation:

What is God speaking to my heart as I read?

_____

_____

_____

_____

_____

_____

TODAY'S *S.O.A.P.* STUDY

Application:

How does this truth apply to my call to follow Jesus?

_____

_____

_____

_____

_____

_____

Prayer:

In light of what God has shown me, how do I need to pray?

_____

_____

_____

_____

_____

_____

Words of Life + Death

"Words are cheap, we say. One picture is worth a thousand words. Silence is golden. But words aren't cheap. They are very precious. They are like water, which gives life and growth and refreshment, but because it has always been abundant, we treat it cheaply."

Katherine Paterson

The tongue has the power of life and death, and those who love it will eat its fruit.—Proverbs 18:21

God's people should use the most life-giving words on the planet. The tongue is a powerful instrument. It encourages the unmotivated and can kill the inspiration of the motivated. The tongue, as a tool, inspires courage. The classic example in the Bible is when Peter walked on water. Jesus not only pastored His disciples, but coached them as well. Jesus coached Peter out of the boat and onto the water with words. After Peter's initial shock wore off, thinking Jesus was a ghost, he wanted to do what he saw his rabbi doing. Although this was not an easy task, Jesus was not about to miss such an opportunity. In order to calm the nerves of the scared disciples, Jesus said, "Take courage! It is I. Don't be afraid." These few words inspired courage in Peter to speak up, "Lord, if it's you…tell me to come to you on the water." All Jesus said was "Come." Jesus' words showed that He believed in Peter. All Peter needed was someone to believe in him in order to do the impossible. If you want to walk on water, then you need someone encouraging you to do so. If you want someone to walk on water, then let your words show him or her that you believe they can do what they think they cannot do.

The tongue, as a weapon, kills motivation. Words of death will immobilize and paralyze the people around you. People will never reach their full potential in life without someone speaking life into their situations. Even in the workplace or the grocery store, the person who negatively speaks about himself or others will lose the right to speak life into others' situations. People unconsciously label you as a person who promotes life or death from the words you speak. When a disaster strikes in someone's life, the last person who will receive a phone call is the person who speaks negatively into every situation. The first person who will receive a call will be the person who is known for always having something life-giving to say. Life-giving speech earns the right to share Christ with people in your workplace, your neighborhood, and your community.

People will always fall short of God's best for their lives if all they hear are words of death. All people have a verbal love tank. It is full of life-giving and life-taking words. Negative words stick like glue. They are hard to erase, but are certainly forgivable. Forgiveness turns words of death into words of life. An apology bridges the gap, while words of death widen it. All people mistakenly speak words of death to their family members, co-workers, neighbors, and those in their community; only people who seek to be life-giving apologize. Always apologize for words of death. Never leave a relationship on death row. Life-giving words encourage the addicted friend to change, the hurting spouse to experience healing, the broken relationship with a neighbor to be restored, and the bad reputation in the community to be positive again. Fishermen catch the most fish with live bait, not dead bait. Make sure your hook always has words of life at the end because you never know when someone will take the bait.

TODAY'S *Community Life* DARE

God dares you to speak life into people's situations. Inspire positive change, and people will always look to you for inspiration. Today, prayerfully resolve to encourage people to do what they think is impossible.

Today's *S. O. A. P.* Study

Scripture:

Proverbs 18:21 Read, Write & Memorize

_____

_____

_____

_____

_____

_____

Observation:

What is God speaking to my heart as I read?

_____

_____

_____

_____

_____

_____

TODAY'S *S.O.A.P.* STUDY

Application:

How does this truth apply to my call to follow Jesus?

_____

_____

_____

_____

_____

_____

Prayer:

In light of what God has shown me, how do I need to pray?

_____

_____

_____

_____

_____

_____

DAY 36
Called to Live

"It's what you are willing to die for which defines you."
Eddie Lawrence

"The thief [Devil] comes only to steal and kill and destroy; I have come that they may have life, and have it to the full. I [Jesus] am the good shepherd. The good shepherd lays down his life for the sheep."—John 10:10-11

God's people should live the most meaningful lives on the planet. Jesus not only taught, but lived the kind of life worth dying for: The kind of life that is worth selling all your possessions for, the kind of life worth denying your selfish dreams for is the kind of life worth losing so that you can gain the life He died for. The life he died for is the only life worth living for today; a life that is passionate about God. Jesus died for a lifestyle that is marked by radical dependence on God and by radical love for others. He lived a life passionate about God so that he could reproduce disciples that would be passionate about God.

The Apostle John, Jesus' most beloved disciple, followed in Jesus' footsteps and lived a life worth dying for by showing passion for God in front of others. He lived the abundant life Jesus calls His followers to embody. History tells us that John discipled a man named Polycarp. Polycarp also became passionate about God to the point that he was unable to live without God. He was asked by the Roman government to deny allegiance to Jesus in exchange for his life, but Polycarp could not. In the face of death, Polycarp said, "Eighty and six years have I served him, and he never once wronged me, how then shall I blaspheme my King, who hath saved me?" He could not fathom living and not being passionate for God. And he was killed for it. John's bait took.

Polycarp was able to choose death as an option because he watched John fish with a life worthy to die for.

John was one of Jesus' first disciples, not Polycarp. John witnessed Jesus' death, not Polycarp. You would think Polycarp would have had to know Jesus personally; you would think that he would have had to experience Jesus' passion for God first hand in order to die for Christianity; but he didn't. Polycarp was discipled by John. He was a second-generation disciple of Christ. Polycarp learned the faith from John who witnessed to the depths of the Christian faith in such a way that Polycarp was willing to die for what he learned by watching the lifestyle of John. John was able to embody Jesus' life and live passionately for God in the presence of Polycarp in such a way that Polycarp replicated John's faith. Polycarp died for the Christianity John modeled for him. If John was a slacker and his witness was not grounded in passion for God, would Polycarp have gone through with martyrdom? The likelihood is slim. Would somebody die because of your life witness? Is your passion for God worth dying for? The fact is, no one has really lived until they have lived the abundant life, a life worth dying for. Live sacrificially until people ask why.

TODAY'S *Community Life* DARE

God dares His followers to live the abundant life, a life passionate about God. Today, make your relationship with God a priority. Live a life worth dying for in front of others; a life of radical dependence on God and extravagant love for others. Today, prayerfully resolve to live the abundant life, a life unlike anything else.

TODAY'S *S. O. A. P.* STUDY

Scripture:

John 10:10-11 Read, Write & Memorize

_____

_____

_____

_____

_____

_____

Observation:

What is God speaking to my heart as I read?

_____

_____

_____

_____

_____

_____

_____

TODAY'S *S.O.A.P.* STUDY

Application:

How does this truth apply to my call to follow Jesus?

_____

_____

_____

_____

_____

_____

Prayer:

In light of what God has shown me, how do I need to pray?

_____

_____

_____

_____

_____

_____

DAY 37
Called to Forgive

"Forgiveness is the key which unlocks the door of resentment and handcuffs of hatred. It breaks the chains of bitterness and the shackles of selfishness. The forgiveness of Jesus not only takes away our sins, it makes them as if they had never been."

Corrie Ten Boom

Then Peter came to Jesus and asked, "Lord, how many times shall I forgive my brother when he sins against me? Up to seven times?" Jesus answered, "I tell you, not seven times, but seventy-seven times."—Matthew 18:21-22

God's people should be the most forgiving people on the planet. The greatest lovers of people are the greatest forgivers. The secret weapon of Christianity is forgiveness. According to Marghanita Laski, one man said, "What I envy most about you Christians is your forgiveness; I have nobody to forgive me." There are people in your work place, neighborhood, and community with the same story. When you fish, throw out your forgiveness lifeline to everyone. Every person who knows you should see you as a person ready to forgive. The greatest fishing stories in Christianity will be attached to moments of great forgiveness. People have little margin in their life for forgiveness. The world wants to see them fail—but when they know there is one person who wants to see them forgiven, that will make a world of difference.

The power of forgiveness is this: "Forgiveness doesn't change the past but it does unlock the future" (author anonymous). The greatest hindrance of future potential in the lives of people is past unforgiveness. People usually find themselves stuck in the present because of past unresolved problems and guilt. Forgiveness does not harp on the past, but focuses on the present. Forgiveness does not rub in people's pain, but helps them rub it out. Those who have been forgiven much can forgive much more in others. That is the mystery of Christianity. God called you into relationship with Him through forgiveness in order for you to be a vessel of forgiveness to others. With God, failure is not final because there is always opportunity to be forgiven by God.

There is an eternal principle that will be valid as long as the world lasts: forgiveness is a costly thing. If you want to impact your neighbor's life, then allow your forgiveness to cost something. Instead of calling the insurance company when your co-worker runs into your car, forgive them. Instead of suing your neighbor when their children ruin your fence, forgive them. It has been said that forgiveness is "giving up my right to hurt you because you have hurt me." Not many people would do what Pope John Paul II did when a lone gunman shot him in St. Peter's Square in 1981. According to Henry Tanner, after surviving extensive surgery and recovering, the Pope went to the jail where his assailant was being held and forgave him for his actions. Forgiveness is never a case of saying: "It's all right; it doesn't matter." As William Barclay said, forgiveness is the most costly thing in the world. Live to forgive, and you will change the people in your world. Forgive people unconditionally until they ask why.

TODAY'S *Community Life* DARE

God dares you to forgive greatly. Teach people how to forgive by asking them for forgiveness. Ask for forgiveness from anyone you have wronged. Forgive anyone who has wronged you. Today, prayerfully resolve to be a person who forgives people no matter how great their sin or how hard their heart.

TODAY'S *S. O. A. P.* STUDY

Scripture:

Matthew 18:21-22 Read, Write & Memorize

_____

_____

_____

_____

_____

_____

Observation:

What is God speaking to my heart as I read?

_____

_____

_____

_____

_____

Today's *S.O.A.P.* Study

Application:

How does this truth apply to my call to follow Jesus?

_____

_____

_____

_____

_____

Prayer:

In light of what God has shown me, how do I need to pray?

_____

_____

_____

_____

_____

DAY 38

Called to Love

*"We never love our neighbor so truly as when our
love for him is prompted by the love of God."*

François Fénelon

*Jesus replied: "Love the Lord your God with all your heart and with all your
soul and with all your mind. This is the first and greatest commandment.
And the second is like it: Love your neighbor as yourself. All the Law and
the Prophets hang on these two commandments."—Matthew 22:37-40*

God's people should be the most loving people on the planet. The
most attractive thing about Jesus was that He did not exclude anybody,
offering His message to everyone equally. He loved the unlovable. The
greater the sin people had in their lives, the greater the love Jesus
showed people. Jesus did not love people because He was forced to—
He wanted to. It was not an obligation, but a privilege for Him. God
gives us specific people at specific times to show His love. God calls us
to love people when they least expect it or deserve it. Loving people is
not a hobby, it's a lifestyle. It is not the last thing to do when you get a
couple extra minutes in your day; it should be the centerpiece of the
day. Love breaks the ice, lowers the defenses and rights any wrongs.
Always show love when you go fishing. It's not a good practice to
throw a hook out without the bait of love attached to it.

Jesus' love for people was the result of His love for God, His Father. He loved people out of a loving relationship with God. Jesus understood that to love people, He had to tap into God, the source of
love. Loving God is a priority issue. Most people are overbooked and
overworked, but under-loved. A lot of times the first thing that falls off
their "to do" list is God. The reality is that no one has accomplished
anything in a day until they have loved God. God must be a priority if
you are going to love people in your home, workplace, neighborhood,

and community. The more you make God a priority, the more people will become a priority. So what could you do less so that you can love God more? The more you love God, the more love you will have for people, and the more people you will love.

Love reels unbelievers in. Love hooks people to God. God has equipped people with a supernatural love that goes the distance. The apostle Paul described love as a verb. He writes, "Love is patient, love is kind. It does not envy, it does not boast, it is not proud. It is not rude, it is not self-seeking, it is not easily angered, it keeps no record of wrongs. Love does not delight in evil but rejoices with the truth. It always protects, always trusts, always hopes, always perseveres. Love never fails..." (1 Corinthians 13:4-8).

If people are loved with anything less than God's supernatural love, a love that does not quit on people when they fail, a love that makes great sacrifices for people even when they crucify you, a love that does not look for returns, a love with no strings attached, then they are not experiencing the unconditional love of God, but the conditional love of people. People are on a hunt for true love. They look far and wide for God's love. Have you properly represented God's love in your sphere of influence? Remember, in the words of Kenneth Boa, "there is no act that begins with the love of God that does not end with the love of our neighbor."

Loving people is also a priority issue. Love people on their terms, on their turf and on their time. When it's convenient for them, not for you. So who can you love that no one else loves? Love people sacrificially until they ask why.

TODAY'S *Community Life* DARE

God dares you to love without returns, without strings attached, and with a supernatural love. Today, prayerfully resolve to make loving God a priority and loving people a habit.

TODAY'S *S. O. A. P.* STUDY

Scripture:

Matthew 22:37-40 Read, Write & Memorize

_____

_____

_____

_____

_____

_____

_____

Observation:

What is God speaking to my heart as I read?

_____

_____

_____

_____

_____

_____

_____

TODAY'S *S. O. A. P.* STUDY

Application:

How does this truth apply to my call to follow Jesus?

_____

_____

_____

_____

_____

_____

Prayer:

In light of what God has shown me, how do I need to pray?

_____

_____

_____

_____

_____

_____

DAY 39

Called to Serve

"Everybody can be great, because anybody can serve. You don't have to have a college degree to serve. You don't have to make your subject and your verb agree to serve. You don't have to know Einstein's theory of relativity to serve. You only need a heart full of grace and a soul generated by love."

Martin Luther King Jr.

Just as the Son of Man did not come to be served, but to serve, and to give his life as a ransom for many. —*Matthew 20:28*

God's people should be the most servant-minded people on the planet. "Unless you are willing to serve Him anywhere, you don't deserve to serve Him anywhere" (author unknown). Jesus served the outcasts, the condemned, and the demon-possessed. He mastered the art of serving the socks off of people! He was on a towel mission. His greatest act of love in His public ministry was His greatest act of service. Jesus showed the fullness of His love for His disciples to settle the "who's the greatest in the Kingdom" argument taking place among His disciples. According to Duane Elmer, they were more concerned with wearing a robe than a towel. They hoped to sit on the right or the left of Jesus when He reigns as King. They wanted the most prestigious positions of power in a kingdom. Wearing the robe meant enjoying the royal status along with the privileges, a big name, prominence, and lots of perks. They wanted to be served.

Like most of us, the disciples did not get it right away, so Jesus had to use a visual reinforcement. Jesus seized the opportunity as they gathered together for the Last Supper by assuming the role of the lowliest servant and doing the unimaginable. He humbly poured water in a basin, wrapping a towel around his waist and without speaking a word He washed the disciples' feet. He even washed the feet of Judas, the disciple who later betrayed Him. Jesus showed them that being great in His kingdom is not the goal, unless it is attained by serving in the Kingdom of God. We serve the King (Jesus), when we serve the King's people. And, as Andy Stanley has said, we love the King, when we love the King's people. If Jesus, our King, made serving a priority, how much more should we, His people, do the same? You have not loved somebody until you have served them.

A four-time, All-Pro NFL linebacker Chris Spielman had played football for twenty-six of his thirty-three years. According to Gary Thomas, Chris met his wife Stefanie in 1983 when he was seventeen. They were married six years later. Stefanie is beautiful—she worked as a model before she became a stay-at-home mom for their two children. Spielman played for many years with the Detroit Lions and signed with the Buffalo Bills in 1996. In 1997, his wife was diagnosed with breast cancer. Stefanie, the beautiful model, opted for a mastectomy, to be followed by six weeks of chemotherapy, during which she would lose her hair. Spielman not only shaved his head, he quit football for the year. This was a defining moment in his life. He said, "Ten years of our entire lives had been about me." He did not want anyone serving his wife but him. Chris Spielman, who isn't even a Christian, did not want anyone out-sacrificing him. In like manner, you should strive to be one of the greatest servants in your family, workplace, neighborhood, or community. Jesus' master plan of evangelism includes serving with no strings attached and serving consistently, not only randomly. Who can you serve that is not being served? Serve people sacrificially until they ask why.

TODAY'S *Community Life* DARE

God dares you to serve the socks off of people. Serving people opens the door for the gospel. Never stop serving people, even if they betray you as Judas did Jesus. Today, prayerfully resolve to show the fullness of God's love by wearing a towel every day, everywhere you go.

Today's *S.O.A.P.* Study

Scripture:

Matthew 20:28 Read, Write & Memorize

_____

_____

_____

_____

_____

_____

Observation:

What is God speaking to my heart as I read?

_____

_____

_____

_____

_____

_____

TODAY'S *S. O. A. P.* STUDY

Application:

How does this truth apply to my call to follow Jesus?

_____

_____

_____

_____

_____

_____

_____

Prayer:

In light of what God has shown me, how do I need to pray?

_____

_____

_____

_____

_____

_____

_____

DAY 40
Called to Give

"When it comes to giving, some people stop at nothing."
Sam Levenson

For God so loved the world that He gave his one and only Son, that whoever believes in Him shall not perish but have eternal life. —*John 3:16*

God's people should be the most giving people on the planet. Jesus was a self-giving person. He gave His all to everyone at all times. There was nothing He held so tightly that He was not willing to give it for the advancement of God's kingdom. He lived with His hands open. When the 5,000 were hungry, He gave them food. When the crowds were suffering, He healed them. When the world needed to be forgiven, He gave His life. Jesus does not expect any more or any less from His followers than radical generosity. Everything He gave was for the purpose of the advancement of the kingdom. God's kingdom moves forward through sacrificial giving of our time, talents, treasures, temple (body), and testimony.

Generosity is a mark of a true disciple. God calls us to give what we have to help others get what they need. Jim Elliot, a missionary who was martyred for his faith, said, "He is no fool who gives what he cannot keep to gain that which he cannot lose." The message of Jesus is more potent when the messenger bears gifts. Sharing the gospel is more effective when we accompany our words with works of love as Jesus did. God could have continued with the impersonal sacrificial system of the Old Covenant to deal with the world's sin, but He chose to personally send His Son not just with the message of forgiveness but also to be the means of forgiveness. The message of Jesus is sacrificial in nature. The message must be accompanied by great sacrifice for the recipients to be greatly impacted. Jesus shared the message of forgiveness everywhere He went and was concerned with people's needs. Who has needs in your workplace, neighborhood, and community that no one is meeting? Some of the most powerful moments of evangelism will be experienced in moments of giving.

The reputation of Christianity rests in your hands. The more followers give, the further the Kingdom of God extends. The giving potential of a follower of Christ is rarely maximized. As Mignon McLaughlin once said, "We'd all like a reputation for generosity, and we'd all like to buy it cheap." Evangelism is not just an exchange of information about the Kingdom of God; it is a sacrifice for the Kingdom of God. Some of the greatest evangelism moments in the office with a co-worker or in the grocery store with a neighbor will be the result of ongoing sacrificial giving. Take the advice of St. Francis of Assisi who said, "Preach the gospel at all times, and when necessary use words." Evangelism is not only about sharing the message of Christ, it is about sharing the sacrificial life of Christ. If people have a hard time understanding Jesus, stop telling them about Him and show them Jesus through your sacrificial giving. Sacrifice as much as possible for the people around you. The less sacrifice attached to the message, the less your message resembles the true message shared by Jesus. Give sacrificially until others ask you why.

TODAY'S *Community Life* DARE

God dares you to give sacrificially. Never allow yourself to be more of a taker than a giver. Give until it hurts, then share Christ. Today, prayerfully resolve to evangelize not only by sharing the message of Jesus' sacrifice, but by giving sacrificially.

TODAY'S *S. O. A. P.* STUDY

Scripture:

John 3:16 Read, Write & Memorize

_____

_____

_____

_____

_____

_____

Observation:

What is God speaking to my heart as I read?

_____

_____

_____

_____

_____

_____

TODAY'S *S.O.A.P.* STUDY

Application:

How does this truth apply to my call to follow Jesus?

_____

_____

_____

_____

_____

_____

Prayer:

In light of what God has shown me, how do I need to pray?

_____

_____

_____

_____

_____

_____

Epilogue

The Revolution
of Discipleship

Taking the risk of discipleship will lead you to the revolution of discipleship. The advancement of the Kingdom of God on earth is through the ongoing process of discipleship. There is not a process on the earth that restores people's lives to wholeness other than the process of following Jesus. Discipleship is the life-transforming process of building God's Kingdom in your home, workplace, neighborhood, and community through partnering with the ministry of the local church. God's revolution of discipleship will not take place apart from your partnership with the local church. If you want to revolutionize the world, then make disciples that make disciples. The local church has done great things for the advancement of the Kingdom of God, but has failed in some ways to fulfill the Great Commission. We have not made disciples who are self-initiating, self-producing, self-feeding, fully devoted followers of Christ. The handoff from one generation of disciples to the next has not been mastered.

One of the most deflating moments for the United States in the history of the Olympic Games occurred in 1988 in Seoul, Korea. The American 4 x 100 relay team was poised to break the world record and assume its position as the best in the world. No one thought that this team could lose. The only question was whether they would break the world record. Yet, as the final leg of the race approached, the unthinkable happened. The Americans dropped the baton. The handoff was not completed. In an instant, the race was over. The crowd, electrified moments earlier, was left in stunned silence. As Greg Ogden points out in his book, *Transforming Discipleship*, American team players had arrogantly relied on their inherent speed and failed to sufficiently practice the handoff that was so crucial for the completion of the race. As William Barclay once said, "Every Christian must see him or herself as the link to the next generation." We must master the handoff in our churches, homes, workplaces, neighborhoods, and communities. All of us must disciple and be discipled. We are the link to the next generation. Daring others to take the 40-day discipleship challenge will build a bridge from this generation to the next. I dare you to practice the handoff by personally walking someone through the 40 days.

ACKNOWLEDGMENTS

First, I thank God for the community of Garden City Church whose passion for discipleship is rare. Your willingness to fully engage in the discipleship process of GCC makes our church a real, reproducing faith community that leads people to become fully devoted followers of Christ who are catalysts of change and examples of human goodness. Thanks for being the guinea pigs!

Second, I want to thank Rev. Rich Cortese, the Senior Pastor of GCC, whose leadership style is rare. He allows me the freedom to think big and dream even bigger. He releases me with resources to turn my thoughts and dreams into reality.

Thirdly, I want to thank the staff of Tremendous Life Books in Mechanicsburg, Pennsylvania, for working diligently to publish this project.

Fourthly, I want to thank Drs. Paul & Virginia Friesen, Marie Sacco, Marissa Frerk, Ron Kline, Elizabeth Urbanek, and "particularly" Graedon Zorzi, seven people who have been extremely committed and instrumental in this project. Marie Sacco, Marissa Frerk, Elizabeth Urbanek, and Graedon Zorzi, the editing team, had their work cut out for them! Ron Kline was the format genius behind this project. Without their help, this project would not read well and look pleasing to the eye!

Lastly, I want to thank my wife, best friend, and discipleship partner, Elizabeth Bousa, whose lifestyle embodies sacrifice, the centerpiece of discipleship. I am immensely indebted to her for her constant support and fervent commitment not just to me, but also to the ministry of the local church. She shapes my life like no one else. She has taught me more about discipleship than I could ever teach her.

ABOUT THE AUTHOR

Jess Bousa is a church planter, author, speaker, and associate pastor of Grace Assembly of God in Bel Air, Maryland. He is a graduate from Teen Challenge Training Center Inc., a faith-based drug and alcohol rehabilitation center, in Rehrersburg, Pennsylvania. He earned his Bachelor of Arts degree in Pastoral Ministry with a minor in Biblical Languages from Valley Forge Christian College in Phoenixville, Pennsylvania. He earned a Master of Arts degree in Biblical Languages and Church Planting from Gordon-Conwell Theological Seminary in South Hamilton, Massachusetts. He is a licensed credential holder with the Assemblies of God. He is the author of *The Discipleship Dare* and *Cultural-Deficit Disorder*. He lives with his beautiful wife, Elizabeth, in Bel Air, Maryland.

Feel free to contact Jess. Though he cannot respond personally to all correspondence, he would love to get your feedback.

Email Jess Bousa:

jjbousa@gmail.com